POLICY AND PRACTICE IN HEALT

NUMBER TEN

LGBT Issues: Looking Beyond Categories

POLICY AND PRACTICE IN HEALTH AND SOCIAL CARE

POLICY AND PRACTICE IN HEALTH AND SOCIAL CARE

SERIES EDITORS

JOYCE CAVAYE and **ALISON PETCH**

LGBT Issues: Looking Beyond Categories

Edited by

Dr Rebecca L. Jones

Lecturer, Faculty of Health and Social Care,
The Open University

and

Dr Richard Ward

Project Worker, School of Nursing, Midwifery and Social Work,
University of Manchester

Published by
Dunedin Academic Press Ltd
Hudson House
8 Albany Street
Edinburgh EH1 3QB
Scotland

ISBN: 978-1- 906716-05-9
ISSN 1750-1407

British Library Cataloguing in Publication data
A catalogue record for this book is available from the British Library

Typeset by Makar Publishing Production, Edinburgh
Printed in the United Kingdom by Cpod, Trowbridge, Wiltshire
Printed on paper from sustainable resources

Contents

Series Editors' Introduction

Article One of the Universal Declaration of Human Rights declares that all humans are born free and equal in dignity and rights – this has particular significance in the context of LGBT individuals and their need for care. LGBT people are real people with real lives, not stereotypes. In terms of access to and participation in health and social care services they are arguably one of the most marginalised groups. LGBT people experience extra barriers in accessing services. Many express dissatisfaction with services citing reasons such as poor communication and common assumptions underpinning practice, such as the assumption that all clients are heterosexual. They are not always open about their sexuality for fear of discrimination or hostility and have a tendency to avoid routine care services. Health and social care practitioners receive little formal training about LGBT issues and thus the unique needs of this client group are often overlooked. Understanding how LGBT people construct their social identity is the first step to providing care that is holistic and appropriate.

This volume provides a refreshing look at the issues surrounding LGBT people. It explores some of the different ways that LGBT identities can be understood in the day-to-day context of care delivery. It questions widely held beliefs that LGBT people are a homogenous group characterised by a fixed set of shared attributes and similar care needs. The authors highlight how the complex and changing ways in which identity labels used by individuals and organisations in care settings can lead to less than optimum care.

Drawing on empirical evidence as well as personal experience, this volume argues collectively that LGBT people are equal in dignity and rights and are entitled to equality of respect and treatment. Care providers must remain aware of the unique issues and health risks of LGBT groups but must also remember to address each service user as an individual. This volume offers vital information, resources and advice for practitioners and policymakers who aspire to deliver high quality person-centred care.

Dr Joyce Cavaye
Faculty of Health and Social Care, The Open University in Scotland, Edinburgh

Professor Alison Petch
*Director, **research in practice** for **adults**, Dartington Hall Trust, Totnes, Devon*

Acknowledgements

The authors would like to thank the Queen Margaret University Multidisciplinary Research Fund for supporting the one-day conference from which this book was developed and all those who attended for their contribution to what proved an exciting and stimulating day. We also wish to thank Tim Hopkins and the Equality Network (www.equality-network.org) for their support and advice in the preparation of this book. Rebecca Jones would additionally like to acknowledge help of various kinds from Helen Bowes-Catton, Doug Clow, Christopher Jones, Jennifer Moore and Esther Saxey. Many thanks are also due to the series editors for their support and helpful feedback throughout the process.

Glossary of Terms

Gender – usually used to denote differences between the sexes that are thought to be socially constructed rather than biological

Gender community – people significantly affected by not fitting mainstream gender rules and assumptions, including trans people and sometimes their partners

Gender dysphoria – distress caused by a conflict between your gender identity and the sex you were assigned at birth

Heteronormativity – the privileging and naturalising of dominant versions of heterosexuality

Heterosexism – the institutionalisation of homophobia that results in the assumed superiority and dominance of opposite-sex relationships and sees other forms as inferior

Intersex – a person whose body is ambiguous with regard to sex

Polyamory – having more than one loving and/or sexual relationship at one time, with the knowledge and consent of all those involved

Queer – a term that has been 'reclaimed' from earlier discriminatory usage, it is used by the many different groups and individuals adversely affected by heteronormativity as a self-identifying description, but is still considered offensive by some

Sex – usually used to denote male/female as defined by bodies, particularly the genitals and secondary sexual characteristics

Trans – inclusive term for wider transsexual, transgender, and sometimes also transvestite, community

Transgender person – someone with a non-traditional view of their sexual or gender identity

Transsexual person – someone who has moved or is moving from one sex/ gender category to another

Contributors

Chrissy Alleyn, former Sexual Dissident at Sussex University, is a Traveller, transactivist, lone parent and independent researcher. Currently involved in queering normative counter-cultural communities and gay spaces in Brighton, sie has a long-range girlfriend and for simplicity's sake describes hirself as 'gender disidentified'.

Carole Archibald, previously a Senior Fieldworker at the Dementia Services Development Centre (DSDC) University of Stirling with main research interests in sexuality and dementia, is now retired and enjoying being a participant observer of what it is to be an older woman in a predominantly youth-focused society. She identifies primarily as female, then heterosexual.

Ann Cronin is a Lecturer in Sociology at the University of Surrey. Her research interests are in ageing, gender and sexuality, especially older LGB adults. While regarding all sexual categories as problematic, she has for the past 22 years identified with the terms lesbian, dyke or queer. She has always identified as a female.

Phil Eaglesham is a Public Health Adviser for NHS Health Scotland and an Associate Lecturer with the Open University. A public health practitioner in HIV, addictions and sexual health, he has research interests that include transgender identity and male sex work. He identifies politically as a gay man with queer tendencies.

John E. Goldring is a Lecturer in Sociology at Manchester Metropolitan University. His research is mainly about gay men's relationships, with each other, their families and friends, and their health and well-being, especially gay men who are marginal to the gay community. He identifies as both gay and male and used to be married.

Rebecca L. Jones is a Lecturer in Health and Social Care at the Open University. Her research interests are mainly in later life, sexuality, and sexuality in later life. She currently identifies as bisexual but has previously thought of herself as 'failed lesbian' and 'mainly straight'. She identifies fairly straightforwardly as female.

Andrew King is a Lecturer in Sociology at Kingston University, London. His research interests are in identity, studies of the life course and sexuality, especially the interrelationship of these topics. He is particularly interested in biographical studies and how people narrate their lives. He has identified himself for all of his adult life as a gay man.

Sara MacKian is a Senior Lecturer in Health and Social Care at the Open University. Her research explores how identity and experience empower or disempower in a range of contexts, including gay men's health, long-term illness, maternal health and contemporary spirituality. Thus far she is confident that she is both a woman and heterosexual.

Richard Ward is a qualified social worker employed by the University of Manchester and Greater Manchester West Mental Health NHS Foundation Trust as a researcher in ageing and mental health. His research interests are in later life, especially dementia, sexuality, appearance, and discrimination. He has followed a trajectory of identifying as outwardly straight, uneasily bisexual and comfortably gay/queer.

Introduction

Richard Ward and Rebecca L. Jones

This book provides a resource for anyone concerned with sexuality and gender identity in health and social care settings. It explores some of the different ways that identities can be understood, focusing particularly on how categories like 'lesbian', 'gay', 'bisexual', and 'trans' are used in everyday care-based encounters. We examine situations in which people use identity labels such as these, and some of the conditions under which they reject or feel constrained by them. The book is intended for practitioners in health and social care who want to become better informed about the implications of LGBT sexual identities in care practice. It is also intended for students, academics and policy makers who wish to add to their knowledge of these issues.

As the title indicates, this book interrogates common understandings of sexuality and gender identity. In doing this, one aim is to question the assumption that LGBT groups or individuals can be readily characterised by a fixed set of shared attributes or needs. For this reason we do not provide a comprehensive overview of issues affecting LGBT people in health and social care settings (for more general introductions to the topic of LGBT issues in health and social care, see Bywater and Jones, 2007; Fish, 2006; Heath and White, 2007; Meyer and Northridge, 2006; Wilton, 2000). Rather, this book demonstrates the complex and changing ways in which identity labels such as these are used by individuals and organisations in care settings.

While the chapters draw on current academic theoretical debate about the nature of identities, we anticipate that at least some of the issues raised may be unfamiliar to many readers. We have therefore grounded the discussion in concrete examples, narratives and case studies. We hope that these will provide specific resources for introducing relevant topics to practice settings and offer guidance toward enhancing current practice.

The changing landscape

The book is being published at a time of significant legislative and policy change in respect to sexuality and gender identity (as outlined in Chapter 1). Much of this change has direct implications and consequences for the care system. Many recent developments are concerned with equalising the rights of different groups and dismantling institutionalised barriers to the access and uptake of welfare services and resources. However, this will only happen in practice if those working at the interface of health and social care possess an awareness of the issues and the capacity to work in an inclusive and supportive fashion. This book is designed to support the development of the relevant skills and understanding in order to begin this process.

Of course, these recent policy developments have come about not in isolation but against the backdrop of steady change in social attitudes to sexuality and associated patterns of living. There is growing evidence of increasingly more positive attitudes to sexual diversity (Scottish Government, 2007) coupled with major changes in the ways that people are choosing to lead their lives. As a result, traditional indicators of sexual difference and gender divisions are becoming increasingly blurred and open to negotiation. The challenge to health and social care lies in being able to adapt and reflect these changes, as well as to serve as an agent for further change and progress, in order to improve the accessibility, appropriateness and effectiveness of care services.

Three approaches to gender identity and sexuality

Much of the discussion in this book surrounds three contrasting but potentially overlapping approaches that might be drawn upon when thinking about sexuality and gender identity in health and social care settings:

- a 'person-centred' approach;
- a 'rights-based' approach;
- a 'deconstructive' approach that draws on ideas taken from Queer Theory.

Each of these approaches has both benefits and limitations, as we now overview.

Person-centred approaches

Person-centred care has become a major focus of health and social care policy in recent years. The Department of Health (e.g. National Service Framework for Older People, 2001) suggests that person-centred approaches are needs-led, involve treating people as individuals, and involve recognising differences. Refocusing care onto the needs and preferences of service users entails looking beyond organisational and institutional categories such as 'older person in need of home care services' or 'person with learning difficulties working in a supported employment scheme'. Instead, it requires service providers to recognise service users as individuals with distinctive life histories, perspectives and values, all of which have implications for the type of services people need. Person-centred care also entails recognising the multiple and overlapping identities and needs which service users may have. For example, a homeless man may also be gay and this may mean that he wants to use a night shelter but finds it has such a homophobic atmosphere that he feels safer sleeping on the streets. In some ways, people who have non-mainstream sexual and gender identities, such as 'lesbian', 'gay man', 'bisexual', 'transsexual' and 'transgender person', can benefit significantly from a person-centred approach. Placing emphasis on people's individuality and personal circumstances is one way that LGBT people can be better served by health and social care services. Sexuality can be addressed at an individual level and as part of a holistic assessment of need that reflects the personal-isation agenda so integral to current health and social care policy.

However, focusing too much on the personal and interpersonal aspects of care can mean that the wider social context is given insufficient attention. Inequalities exist at broader levels than those of individual use of services. Person-centred care can be in danger of locating problems with care services at the level of individuals only – framing the issue as one of a particular care worker's attitudes or lack of training, or a particular service user's situation or history. It can distract from also looking at organisational and institutional factors in the situation. For example, if you just focus on an individual gay homeless man and his situation and needs, you may not see a potential need for organisational change such as a specialised service for LGBT homeless people.

Rights-based approaches

An emphasis on the broader social and institutional discrimination faced by LGBT people was a key focus of LGBT activist work from the 1960s onwards.

Partly due to the legacy of this work, public policy and legislation has brought LGBT issues into new prominence, not least in health and social care (as discussed in Chapter 1). The mainstreaming of this approach concentrates on protection against discrimination and creating fairer conditions, often via the legal system, and duties placed upon different public agencies and institutions. This has created a new climate in which there is much greater emphasis upon public services becoming accessible and inclusive of LGBT people. This extends to individuals working within health and social care services, who may be expected to be aware of LGBT issues in a way that was not previously the case.

However, such an approach depends upon individuals identifying under particular labels, such as 'lesbian' or 'transsexual'. As many of the chapters in this book demonstrate, there may be various reasons why some people do not subscribe to these familiar labels, and so may not take up services if they do not recognise them as appropriate for themselves. Approaches that treat sexual and gender identities as fixed and homogenous can also create difficulties, as will become apparent.

Deconstructive approaches

Another development in ways of thinking about sexuality and gender identities that is central to this book is 'Queer Theory'. This way of thinking about categories such as 'woman', 'man', 'lesbian' or 'heterosexual' is based particularly on the work of commentators such as Judith Butler (e.g. 1993), Steven Epstein (e.g. 1987), Steven Seidman (e.g. 1996) and Michael Warner (e.g. 1991). In one sense, this more deconstructive approach is compatible with person-centred care in that it builds on the idea that people are very individual and different. It draws attention to the way in which there is actually lots of variation within what we assume to be a group with shared features. One 'homeless gay man' can be so different from another that it becomes unhelpful and even counter-productive to think of them as belonging to a group. Queer Theory suggests that categories such as 'a woman', 'a man', 'a lesbian' or whatever have become so powerful that they seem natural and inevitable, but actually they are not. Butler and other Queer Theorists argue that identities are not pre-existing but constantly performed in everyday life: not who you essentially are, but what you do. Individuals can identify in multiple ways over time and across different situations. This idea is applicable to lots of types of identity, such as 'Scot', 'older person' and so on, but has been particularly developed in relation to sexual and gender identities.

As will become apparent in some of the chapters in this book, this radical rethinking challenges the very idea of the categories 'lesbian', 'gay', 'bisexual' and 'trans' in a way that can be simultaneously both helpful and challenging to health and social care practice.

However, this way of thinking about identity categories is still unfamiliar to many people, so it can seem too far removed from everyday practices to be useful (although we hope some of the chapters in this book will demonstrate that this is not necessarily the case). The other difficulty with Queer Theory approaches is that their emphasis on difference and the instability of identity labels can make it more difficult to organise politically, to recognise common problems and needs, and to design care services to respond to those needs.

Each of these three approaches might usefully be thought of as part of a toolkit, offering different resources and strategies for thinking about and negotiating issues of sexuality and gender identity. The chapters in this book explore these approaches in ways that are grounded in practical illustrations and examples, and supported by critical analysis. A key concern is to support a better understanding of both the merits and limitations associated with each approach.

Outline of the book

The over-arching aim of this book is to support readers in developing a critical approach to sexualities and gender identities in health and social care practice. Having considered the existing material on sexuality and gender identity in health and social care we have sought to address what we see as four important gaps in the literature.

Firstly, this book takes account of the growing devolvement of powers from central government to the different countries that make up the UK, focusing particularly on the situation in Scotland. In Chapter 1, Phil Eaglesham overviews recent policy and legislation affecting LGBT people in health and care services. He pays particular attention to research and policy that is particular to Scotland. In Chapter 3, Carole Archibald presents empirical data collected in Scotland.

Secondly, the existing literature is also characterised by an emphasis upon younger groups and associated issues. This is due, in part, to historical patterns of funding that have been available to research and practice in the field of health care, but is also due to an assumption that sexuality is an issue affecting younger but not older people (Gott, 2004). As a response to this, the book contains chapters that consider the perspectives of older LGBT people.

In Chapter 2, Sara MacKian and John Goldring explore the significance of generational differences in gay men's use of gay space to the success of health promotion campaigns. In Chapter 3, Carole Archibald presents the findings from her Scottish study of the views of older lesbians about their future care needs. In the final chapter of the book, Ann Cronin and Andrew King use the example of older LGB carers to examine the heteronormativity of care identities.

Thirdly, existing resources tend to offer information primarily on lesbian and gay issues with only limited or tokenistic reference to the 'B' (bisexual) and 'T' (trans) in LGBT. In Chapter 4, Rebecca Jones overviews some of the ways bisexuality complicates sexual and gender identity categories in care settings. In Chapter 5, Chrissy Alleyn and Rebecca Jones introduce 'dissident' trans identities, discuss how they relate to more 'traditional' transsexual identities and draw out the implications of this for care practices.

Fourthly and finally, the book is distinguished from much else that exists in this field by seeking to look beyond these familiar categories and consider, at a much broader level, the culture of health and social care. It highlights the responsibilities and the challenges that exist for all those who work in and use the care system and shows that we are all implicated in this culture irrespective of how we might identify at an individual level.

CHAPTER 1

The Policy Maze and LGBT Issues: Does One Size Fit All?

Phil Eaglesham

Introduction

Public policy can be an important means of addressing both direct and indirect discrimination to protect minority and vulnerable citizens. As a gay man, I benefit enormously from the inclusion that this brings to living in Scotland. In this chapter I will provide an overview of the key policies and legislation that benefit all LGBT people and reflect on my own experience as an 'out' gay Scottish man. I will consider the extent to which research has helped foster inclusion and suggest future opportunities for evidence gathering on LGBT needs. Finally I will challenge the expectation that such 'one size' policy can genuinely include and 'fit all' when limitation exists in the commonly used categories within LGBT issues.

The impact of LGBT discrimination on society and the individual

Homophobia (Avert, 2008; Thompson, 1998), biphobia (Mulick and Wright, 2002; Ochs, 1996) and transphobia (Thompson, 1998), as with all forms of discrimination, can impact directly in a range of settings, through barriers to access, education, employment, training, promotion, goods and services and through frank exclusion and dismissal. It can also occur in covert ways, often more readily perceived by the LGBT person than others (Scottish Government, 2008a). Indirectly, this discrimination operates in the workplace through organisational policies, rules, recruitment, selection and admission. This can occur through assumption, for example regarding the gender in partnerships or entitlement to parental or compassionate leave and in such situations through the absence of clear means or access to complaint (*Employment Equality (Sexual Orientation) Regulations*: OPSI, 2003). In more extreme cases, such harassment and victimisation affects the individual's dignity, interferes with learning or induces fear, stress or sickness. In these ways, whether overt or subtle, homophobia, biphobia and transphobia are blatantly bad for the health and well-being of both individuals and communities, inflicting damage upon the Scottish and UK economies (Stonewall, 2003).

More than half of my life has been spent as an openly gay man. My gay male identity has also been informed by the range of political, social and health factors that have affected the lives of all LGBT people in Scotland. My own political awareness however, emerged earlier in my life. Anti-racism, anti-Thatcherism and the class struggle of the miners' strike in the 1980s triggered my earliest sense of outrage and led me to join marches and demonstrations. These experiences fuelled my 'post-out' contribution to the struggle for equality and fostered my acute awareness of the impact of homophobia. Several challenges have arisen in the years since I 'came out' and the Scottish policy response to these has reassured me that Scotland not only strives for but is moving forward to become a fairer, more equal society by increasingly researching, challenging and outlawing discrimination. In this struggle, I recall the many Scottish LGBT champions who have fallen and 'passed over the rainbow' or been thwarted by discrimination. I am reassured, however, that LGBT people in Scotland now have enormous potential to thrive. In the following sections, I will firstly discuss the social history that prompted change and then detail the key Scottish policies that aimed to promote equality for LGBT people.

The struggle for equality: recent LGBT history in Scotland

Key elements of Scottish society have traditionally displayed a pervasive culture of homophobia, fostered by patriarchal institutions and some forms of organised religion (Cant, 2008; Whyte, 1995). While the decriminalisation of homosexuality between men over 21 in England and Wales occurred in 1967, it would be a further 13 years of debate and political struggle before Robin Cook MP amended the Criminal Justice (Scotland) Bill in 1980 for an equal law in Scotland (Kellas, 1989). During this time however, LGBT Centres, lesbian, gay and trans 'Switchboard' help-lines, bookshops, support projects and vibrant LGBT art and culture emerged to meet the needs that mainstream society (and core health and social services) were unable or unwilling to provide for. For those daring to come out, these were politically charged and exciting times.

LGBT activists in Scotland also challenged injustice through the Scottish Minorities Group. Formed in 1969, it evolved into the Scottish Homosexual Rights Group in 1978 and produced the magazine *Gay Scotland* (Cant, 2008). In the 1980s, which hosted my personal 'coming out', Section 28 was introduced to prevent the 'promotion' of homosexuality by local authorities in Great Britain (Equality Network, 2000) and in 1987, consenting sado-masochistic acts were criminalised under the law of assault in England and Wales through the targeting of gay men in the notorious 'Spanner' case (Spanner Trust, 2008). This perhaps indicated how out of step the police and legal establishment were with changing attitudes to sex and sexuality among some sections of society. This occurred at a time when fear and ignorance of HIV ran high and the epidemic began killing thousands of gay and bisexual men in the UK (Avert, 2008). During these Thatcherite years however, Stonewall Youth, Glasgow LGBT Centre and the Glasgay! festival were all launched in Scotland and the Lesbian Archive and Information Centre (LAIC), set up in London in 1984, relocated into the Glasgow Women's Library (OurStory Scotland, 2008). Hopes for equality were dashed in 1994 when Parliament voted to only reduce the gay male age of consent to 18 (rather than 16). Although HIV/AIDS ravaged the LGBT community during these years, many were politically active and increasingly focused on preventing HIV along with combating the homophobia, biphobia and transphobia then often prevalent within the UK.

As the Conservative Party's rule of the UK ended and the millennium approached, the 1997 referendum that helped create the Scottish Parliament provided LGBT people with an unprecedented opportunity to benefit from devolved power. The Equality Network was formed in 1997 and that year Health Gay Scotland was launched as the first Scottish health promotion initiative to focus on sexual health and HIV for gay and bisexual men. Earlier struggles appeared to dissipate as the Scottish Parliament made dramatic progress in tackling discrimination in law. The almost immediate repeal of Section 2A (commonly referred to as Clause 28) defeated a well-orchestrated media campaign by a homophobic and evangelical Christian lobby funded by businessman Brian Souter (Equality Network, 2008). This sent a clear signal that Scotland would create a more open and equal society and since then LGBT rights have been recognised in Scottish legislation within a wide range of mainstream policies. In the next section I will consider the scale of this LGBT-related policy in the UK and Scotland.

Fostering equality: LGBT citizenship in the UK

In the UK, but especially in Scotland, a comprehensive approach to legislation has evolved to protect many (but not all) LGBT citizens across a range of different areas of their lives. The banning of discrimination against LGBT people under UK legislation was prompted by our membership of the European Union (EU) (Equality Network, 2008). The European Court of Justice also ruled in 1998 that EU laws that ban sex discrimination also applied to transsexual people. The Sex Discrimination Act was then updated to protect transsexual people from discrimination within employment or in the provision of vocational training (Department for Education and Employment, 1999). In 2000 the EU agreed a directive also banning discrimination in employment and vocational training on grounds of sexual orientation, religion and belief, disability and age (Official Journal of the European Communities: 2000/78/EC). As a result, the UK introduced Employment Equality (Sexual Orientation) Regulations (OPSI, 2003) to outlaw such discrimination on the grounds of sexual orientation. The Gender Recognition Act (OPSI, 2004a) also became law in 2004 to ensure that, subject to certain conditions, a person who has a diagnosis of gender dysphoria can apply for a gender recognition certificate as their new sex, giving them complete legal recognition in that gender (Press for Change, 2008). Transsexual campaigners have successfully utilised European law, particularly within the workplace setting, to foster equality in the UK.

The Equality Act (OPSI, 2006) established a single UK Commission for Equality and Human Rights to combat discrimination on the grounds of sex, disability, race, religion and belief, sexual orientation, gender reassignment and age. This introduced a public sector 'gender equality duty' and ensured protection from discrimination on the grounds of religion and belief with regards to goods, facilities, services and public functions. Examples include services in shops or pubs, accommodation in guesthouses, treatment by NHS services, and access to school education. This also gave the UK parliament the power to introduce similar regulations to protect against direct or indirect discrimination on the grounds of sexual orientation through the Equality Act (Sexual Orientation) Regulations (OPSI, 2007). A further EU Gender Directive (Council of the European Union: 2004/113/EC) required the UK to ban discrimination in 2004 against transsexual people in the supply of goods, facilities and services. The Sex Discrimination (Amendment of Legislation) Regulations (OPSI, 2008) therefore passed into law. These specific legislative protections for LGBT people developed in an increasingly mainstream environment to enhance equality.

In 2004 the Civil Partnerships Act (OPSI, 2004b) created the new legal relationship in the UK of 'civil partnership', formed when two people of the same sex sign a registration document. This also provides parity of treatment in a wide range of legal matters with those opposite-sex couples who enter into a marriage. When married or cohabiting mixed-sex couples receive artificial insemination treatment at a licensed fertility clinic, both partners are regarded as the legal parents of the child born as a result. However, until very recently, if a same-sex female couple (whether civil partners or cohabiting) received treatment, only the woman who became pregnant was regarded as the child's parent – her partner was not. Since the Human Fertilisation and Embryology Act 2008 (Department of Health, 2007) came into effect in 2009, the female partner of a woman receiving treatment at a licensed clinic in the UK can be recognised as the child's second parent. If the women are civil partners, this will also apply where conception is by 'DIY' donor insemination (i.e. not done at a clinic). While in recent years many LGBT people have chosen to form informal co-habiting and co-parenting relationships, the law now offers them better protection in seeking to promote equality. Heteronormative assumptions of what constitutes 'marriage' and a 'family' therefore may not legally apply in the 21st century UK with regard to committed civil partnerships. These may not, however, capture the living arrangements that many LGBT people choose to adopt in their closest relationships. In Scotland, a range of further legislation has been developed to acknowledge both civil partnerships and informal relationships and these are detailed in the next section.

Devolved equality: LGBT citizenship in Scotland

While the power to shape equalities legislation remains reserved to the UK parliament at Westminster, several devolved legislative changes have benefited Scottish LGBT people. This section summarises many of the key areas of impact and equality. The Adults with Incapacity (Scotland) Act (Scottish Executive, 2000) states that a partner of someone in a same-sex relationship can be treated as that person's nearest relative, in the same way as a husband or wife. The Housing (Scotland) Act (Scottish Executive, 2001a) entitles same-sex partners to succeed tenancy when a partner dies and the Mortgage Rights (Scotland) Act (Scottish Executive, 2001b) grants same-sex partners the right to apply for a court order to stop a property being repossessed. The Criminal Justice (Scotland) Act (Scottish Executive, 2003b) recognises same-sex partners as victim's partners and supports participation in the criminal justice process, including information-giving and support for victims of crime. That same year the Civil Legal Aid (Scotland) Amendment Regulations (Scottish Executive 2003a) recognised the right of same-sex partners, who are living together in a relationship 'which has the characteristics of the relationship between husband and wife', to be treated as if they were spouses in assessment of resources. The Mental Health (Care and Treatment) (Scotland) Act (Scottish Executive, 2003c) recognised that same-sex partners may count as nearest relatives, equal to partners of the opposite sex. More recently, the Family Law (Scotland) Act (Scottish Executive, 2006b) gave new rights to cohabiting couples, including same-sex partners, regarding inheritance and financial provision after relationship breakdown, and the Adoption and Children (Scotland) Act 2007 (Scottish Executive, 2006a) was passed by the Scottish Parliament. Since July 2009, a cohabiting same-sex couple who are in 'an enduring family relationship' have been able to apply to jointly adopt a child, and one partner is now able to apply to 'step-parent' adopt their partner's child. Wider protection for those in same-sex relationships has therefore slowly delivered equality in many of the basic laws that govern Scotland.

An integrated equality and diversity approach across many health policies has also developed within NHS Scotland, closely aligned with 'Patient Focus and Public Involvement' (Scottish Executive, 2001c). This aims to ensure accessible, appropriate and non-discriminatory NHS services, responsive to the individual circumstances of people's lives. Health policies such as Partnership for Care (Scottish Executive, 2003d), the NHS Reform (Scotland) Act (OPSI, 2004c) and Fair for All – The Wider Challenge (SEHD, 2004) all challenge direct or indirect discrimination towards LGBT people within healthcare settings. Within the criminal justice system there is a similar need to ensure equality. In 2009, a bill proposed by 'out' Green Party MSP Patrick Harvie, the Offences (Aggravation by Prejudice) (Scotland) (Scottish Parliament, 2008) passed into law. This means that when passing sentence on a hate crime, a motive of prejudice relating to disability, sexual orientation or transgender identity can now be taken into account in a similar way to racial or religious motivation by attackers.

Beyond UK legislation, further progress has been made across life circumstances to legislate for an equal Scottish society and protect the rights of sexual minorities. However, not all LGBT people are protected by such legislation and while equality in part has been achieved, Scotland may not have truly acknowledged the diversity that exists within gender and sexual identities or the strength of evidence that shapes this. I will now explore some of the useful LGBT research studies and reports that have informed policy in Scotland.

LGBT research and 'evidence into policy'

The work of LGBT researchers and those with a concern for the interests and well-being of LGBT groups and individuals has been a key component of the struggle for equality. In this section I will discuss how health inequality has been identified, described and explained in order to encourage government to address the isolation, abuse and exclusion that some LGBT people experience. In providing the evidence to support this, research has also encouraged statutory and voluntary sector action to provide tailored practice solutions to LGBT people. Innovative research on rarely studied groups and newly considered health needs, for example on male sex workers (Connell and Hart, 2003), has occurred within Scotland. Much of this is not peer-reviewed and resides within the policy and voluntary sectors, so would be classified as 'grey literature'. Several of these studies and reports, however, provide evidence of a community in isolation and at times in crisis. While scientific and epidemiological evidence has informed practitioners and services, a further range of evaluations, surveys and qualitative studies have also impacted on policy and practice in Scotland and the UK. Although the evidence base on LGBT health lacks robust and systematic review in a Scottish or UK context, several surveys, research reports and descriptive studies have contributed to policies and strategies that improve health and promote equality.

A survey by the Beyond Barriers project (carried out by Stonewall in 2002) of the LGBT population in Scotland recruited 924 participants at events, through an online focus group and via an online questionnaire. The project report, *First Out* (Bell and Morgan, 2003), includes LGBT profiles, and discusses issues of personal safety and access to both information and healthcare. Of the respondents, 15% reported difficulty in accessing mainstream health care. The main reasons given by respondents were 'inappropriate advice' and 'homophobic GP or practice staff'. In this survey, 68% of respondents reported being verbally abused or threatened within their lifetime because someone assumed they were LGBT, 35% within the previous year. In Glasgow a survey of young gay, lesbian and bisexual people, *Something To Tell You* (Coia et al., 2002), opportunistically recruited 122 people under 25 from LGB organisations and a variety of LGBT spaces. Only 20% of respondents reported that they had *not* experienced discrimination and 43% of young women and 20% of young men reported having been diagnosed with depression. While this report did not claim to be representative of the LGB population in Scotland, the survey indicated that a substantial number of young people may have experienced direct homophobic discrimination. A further report, *Live to Tell* (Gay Men's Health, LGBT Youth Scotland, 2003), presents findings from a study on suicidal thoughts, feelings and behaviours among young gay and bisexual men in Edinburgh. These support the findings from UK-wide research on higher levels of psychological distress and experiences of discrimination among LGBT people (King *et al.*, 2003; Warner *et al.*, 2004). Transphobic harassment and barriers to services are also described in *Transgender experiences in Scotland* (Scottish Transgender Alliance / Equality Network, 2008). This survey found that 25% of 71 respondents stated that they have previously had to move home (often becoming homeless) and 62% of respondents had experienced transphobic harassment from strangers in public places who perceived them to be transgender.

Scottish research studies have mainly focused on LGBT sexual health and the epidemiology of HIV and AIDS among gay men in particular (Stonewall, 2003). Some more recent studies have also examined mental health, screening uptake, smoking and alcohol use. Recruiting a representative sample of LGBT people is always a challenge. Many researchers rely on convenience sampling, making it more difficult to generalise findings to wider LGBT health. Studies have identified sexual risk among gay, bisexual men and other 'men who have sex with men' (MSM) associated with HIV (Hart and Williamson, 2005; Williamson and Hart, 2007; Yirrell *et al.*, 2004) and other sexually transmitted infections such as syphilis and hepatitis B (Knussen and Flowers, 2007; McMillan, 2006; Palmer and Young, 2006; Young *et al.*, 2006). This has also been informed by high quality descriptive research, the majority based on surveys (Knussen *et al.*, 2004 ; Hart and Williamson, 2005; Williamson *et al.*, 2008). Qualitative research studies based on interview and focus group work with MSM also contribute through reports and briefings within 'grey literature' (Burtney and Hosie / HIV Scotland, 2007; Hunt *et al.* / Stonewall, 2007). These have informed on the health behaviours that contribute to the prevalence of sexually transmitted diseases and also appear to have considered community activism (Hart *et al.*, 2004) as a means to meet the needs of MSM and strengthen the policy imperative for equality in Scotland.

As depressing as the statistics can often appear, the surveillance that Scotland has developed in monitoring sexually transmitted infections is among the best in the world. In considering wider sexual health, the report *Moving Forward* (Health Protection Scotland, 2005) described patterns of sexually transmitted infections in Scotland using information from laboratories, genitourinary medicine clinics, primary care and HIV surveillance. This has continued with the publication of *Sexually Transmitted Infections and Other Sexual Health Information for Scotland* (Health Protection Scotland, 2007). These reports have considered sexual behaviour in order to understand patterns of infection and focused on MSM, among other vulnerable groups, highlighting three infections of particular concern: gonorrhoea, syphilis and HIV. In 2006 there were 147 new cases of HIV among Scottish MSM, the highest number ever found among this group in Scotland. Cases of syphilis, including co-infection with chlamydia, gonorrhoea and HIV, have also increased sharply in recent years. This has mobilised services and researchers to attempt to predict and better understand health behaviour, particularly among gay men.

The Medical Research Council's Social and Public Health Sciences Unit has conducted the Gay Men's Sexual Health Survey in Scotland every 3 years since 1996. This provides lifestyle and sexual behaviour data through use of surveys and HIV screening in the bars, clubs and LGBT spaces that gay men helped create (Williamson and Hart, 2007). While prevention of new HIV infection among MSM remains a research focus in Scotland, a study of Scottish lesbian women attending a sexual health clinic (Carr *et al.*, 1999) found that 40% of 200 survey respondents were not 'out' to their GP and attendees presented with untreated gynaecological and fertility issues (52%), psychosocial problems (26%) and genitourinary conditions (20%). This evidence of poor health supports findings from previous UK studies (Bailey et al, 2003, Fish *et al.*, 2007) and a recent UK-level health-check survey of over 6000 lesbian and bisexual women, *Prescription for Change* (Hunt and Fish, 2008). The latter reported higher levels of substance use, poor uptake of cancer screening and sexual health services and poorer mental health combined here with experiences of direct discrimination, domestic violence between women and histories of attempted suicide. Transgender people have also reported poor confidence in knowledge and attitudes among NHS staff in general practice, mental health and out of hours support, although sexual health services often compare more favourably (Scottish Transgender Alliance, 2008). This echoes UK-level evidence of transgender NHS service users (Whittle *et al.*, 2007).

While this research and survey data indicate poorer LGBT health, the overall lack of robust evidence on these groups remains a cause for concern. It may be difficult to establish causal links, but the health inequalities of LGBT people continue to make stark reading. High quality survey research is used by all levels of government to inform policy on a range of health issues. The sources of evidence relied upon, however, are not representative of the true health and social care needs of LGBT people and do not capture the impact of discrimination on health behaviours. The next section will consider data sources on LGBT people.

Improving the data sources on LGBT people

Scottish population-based health survey results are increasingly being used to monitor health and social care targets set by government and such surveys should collect information about the sexual orientation of respondents to ensure they are truly representative. A large number of sample surveys of people, households and businesses are conducted at a UK level and include Scottish data which, although not representative, will increasingly incorporate LGBT data to support policy on equality (see Table 1.1).

Information on LGBT people used to inform policy can be gathered from sources such as the 2006 Scottish Social Attitudes (SSA) survey on discriminatory attitudes towards disabled people, women, minority ethnic groups, and LGBT people. While the survey results showed encouraging signs of less prejudice towards lesbians and gay men, it was particularly common for discrimination against transgender people to be voiced. In *Towards a Healthier LGBT Scotland* (Stonewall, 2003), the NHS used evidence from the previous SSA survey in 2002 to develop its Inclusion Project in 2002 and created a web-based LGBT research database on health and well-being under the banner of *Fair For All* (SEHD, 2004). In response to population survey findings, the Scottish Executive funded the Sexual Orientation Research Project in 2003 with three distinct phases. It reviewed methodological approaches (McManus, 2003) and captured the perspectives of LGBT community organisations (McLean and O'Connor, 2003). It then carried out a stock-take of local authority policy and practice and produced guidance to support this (Fyfe *et al.*, 2006).

Promoting the use of such evidence to improve the planning of services, the Scottish Government also developed the Portal to Resources and Information on Mainstreaming Equality (PRIME; Scottish Government 2008b), a collection of equality-related (web-based) resources, helping policy makers and researchers understand the range of equality issues (including sexual orientation) and their relevance across policy areas. The themes explored there

Data Sources on LGBT People in Scotland	Useful Surveys Conducted in Scotland	Further Surveys Conducted at UK Level
Scottish Workforce Information Standard System (SWISS): *collects information about the sexual orientation of those employed within the NHS in Scotland for the purposes of monitoring discrimination and equal opportunities policy.*	Scottish Household Survey: *Up-to-date information on the characteristics, attitudes and behaviour of Scottish households on a range of issues.*	General Household Survey: *Data on five core topics: education, employment, health, housing, population and family.*
The National Survey of Sexual Attitudes and Lifestyles 2000: *collected information from the British population (including Scotland) and includes information about cohabitation history; types of homosexual or heterosexual experience and number of partners.*	Scottish Health Survey: *A wide range of health information.*	Labour Force Survey: *Range of information on the UK labour market.*
Office for National Statistics (ONS): *Their website contains information about uptake of civil partnerships since the legislation was introduced including monthly and quarterly data by area of formation, sex and age at formation.*	Scottish Crime and Victimisation Survey: *The experience, and the perception, of crime and policing in Scotland.*	New Earnings Survey: *Information on the earnings of employees in businesses of all kinds and sizes.*
Scotland's Census Results On Line (SCROL): *In 2002 it recorded the number of people who reported living with someone of the same sex: table UV49*	Scottish House Condition Survey: *The physical condition of houses and interviews with the people who live in them.*	Expenditure and Food Survey: *Information on household expenditure on goods and services as well as household income.*
Scottish Social Attitudes Survey (SSA): *The 2002 survey included questions on discriminatory attitudes towards disabled people, women, minority ethnic groups and gay men and lesbians.*	Public Attitudes to the Environment in Scotland Survey: *Survey of Public Attitudes to the Environment in Scotland.*	Family Resources Survey: *Information on household's resources and income.*

Source: Scottish Public Health Observatory: www.scotpho.org.uk

Table1.1: Surveys Conducted in Scotland and at UK Level

indicate the scale of the policy maze that those advocating for LGBT people must navigate. Justice, arts and culture, education, training, employment and housing are policy areas where researchers and civil servants in Scotland can use PRIME to consider potential equality implications. More recently, the recommendations of the Hearts and Minds' Agenda Group (Scottish Government, 2008a) on challenging LGBT discrimination in the workplace have the potential to impact across a range of other social issues such as faith and beliefs, education, family life and the media, and to promote active citizenship. In their recommendations, cross-cutting themes from the Hearts and Minds agenda included commissioning LGBT research, establishing equality and respect as a cornerstone of a modern, successful country and a more strategic approach to LGBT inclusion and participation, which in turn provide more accurate information on LGBT people's health and social care needs. In delivering these changes, a wide range of professional groups could potentially contribute to the future evidence base on LGBT people across a number of health and social care themes in Scotland (see Table 1.2).

Table 1.2: Sources of Support for LGBT Health and Wellbeing

HEALTH AND SOCIAL SECTORS	PROFESSIONAL GROUPS
Housing	Social Work
Health	Teaching
Education	Nursing
Criminal Justice	Medicine
Public Services	Allied Professionals
Discrimination	Housing
Cohabitation	Advocacy
Parenting	Community
Partnerships	Police
Immigration	Legal
	Leisure Services

To be effective, public services should also consider evidence beyond policy and published academic literature. While published journal articles and academic reviews can influence policy and service decisions, their transferability and effectiveness in local settings may not be successful. Some theory-based interventions that practitioners tacitly know make a difference to individuals may have no formal evaluation evidence to support their use but greatly benefit service users (Pawson et al., 2003). Considering the constraints on academic evidence and the slow process by which it emerges, a more pragmatic approach might be required if the urgent needs of LGBT people are to be met. There is a need to collaborate on studies that 'do good', strengthen equity and ensure an ethical approach throughout.

Can 'one size' fit all for equality and diversity in Scotland?

Use of the *Equality and Diversity Impact Assessment Toolkit* (Scottish Executive, 2005) for policy and planning can sensitise services when combined with training that increases the skill of professionals to support LGBT people. Does such a tool really improve public sector performance and does the range of identities that it claims to address include everyone? Can 'one size' fit all? Currently it only incorporates legislation and policy that considers the needs of certain key sexual identities (see Table 1.3).

Table 1.3: Current gender and sexual identities considered within Scottish and UK Legislation

Lesbian Women
Gay Men
Bisexual Women
Bisexual Men
Transsexual Straight Men
Transsexual Bisexual Men
Transsexual Lesbian Women
Transsexual Bisexual Women
Transsexual Straight Women
Transsexual Gay Men

While an LGBT alliance has emerged to seek justice and equality, the health needs, social imperatives and political perspectives among these four distinct groups can vary considerably. Lesbian and bisexual women's lives may be informed by feminist theory and culture which appears considerably different from the aspiring, hedonistic lifestyle portrayed in commercial gay male culture. When faced with a range of needs and perspectives, many services will be challenged if their awareness is based only on the existence of the commercial gay and lesbian scene as discussed by MacKian and Goldring within this book. Gay men and lesbian women may often identify differently in their political or social outlook, and a range of sub-cultures (Atkinson and Hammersley, 1994) has evolved to further extend intra-group differences and division. Bisexual people are often ignored or stigmatised by such groups and further removed still are the perspectives of transsexual people who may develop a range of sexual and gender identities. How inclusive is the term LGBT then in capturing human sexuality? If an individual does not choose one of the above prescribed categories, will exclusion persist and equality remain elusive? Much of the legislation that governs the well-being of transgender people, for instance, is specific to those who identify as transsexual and are undergoing gender reassignment surgery. Is this the only (biomedical) route to equality and justice? This specific issue is discussed in Alleyn and Jones's chapter in this book. Table 1.4 lists further gender and sexual identities that are potentially excluded from Scottish and UK legislation, implying that some LGBT people may be less equal than others.

Figure 1.4: Further gender and sexual identities, potentially excluded from Scottish and UK Legislation.

Intersexual Gay Men
Intersexual Straight Men
Intersexual Bisexual Men
Intersexual Lesbian women
Intersexual Bisexual Women
Intersexual Straight Women
Polygender Straight Men
Polygender Bisexual Men
Polygender Lesbian women
Polygender Bisexual Women
Polygender Straight Women
Men and women who cross dress or identify as transvestite.

Overlay this with other multiple needs on disability, ethnicity, age and beliefs and the challenge to services can seem enormous and insurmountable. Can 'one size' truly fit all? While discrimination and hate crime are more often directed at gay men and transgender women (Scottish Executive, 2003e), all LGBT people suffer whether discrimination occurs directly or indirectly. Homophobia, biphobia and transphobia affect the whole of society. They impact with degrees of both 'chronic' and 'acute' intensity at key life stages. It may be better for services to focus on the *severity* of discrimination at key *life stages* and *life experiences* rather than attempting to offer broad interventions that might fail to address unique individual needs within sexuality and gender. Further examples where new ways of categorising LGBT people have emerged to challenge our preconceptions include the efforts of a US social marketing agency (New American Dimensions/Asterix Group, 2007) to create a 'sub-grouping' of LGBT people that can be used to target advertising and products (see Table 1.5).

While the purpose of this is commercial, it suggests a model beyond the accepted 'four spheres' of LGBT. It is hierarchical in the extreme, appearing

Table 1.5: Terms used in American social marketing theory to target LGBT people

'Super Gays' – most aware of gay identity and the most conscious of anti-gay discrimination.

'Habitaters' – in long-term relationships and are primarily concerned with domestic issues like children and health care.

'Gay Mainstream' – mix their interest in gay issues and media with mainstream concerns.

'Party People' – the most cutting edge and urban in their tastes and the most likely to spend money on personal pampering.

'Closeted' – older, living in small towns and aren't likely to have many gay friends or belong to LGBT organizations.

(New American Dimensions /Asterix Group (2007) 'Real World Lesbians & Gays')

to favour the richest and most 'style aware' over those who might be isolated and potentially vulnerable. Relationships, location, family life, politics and identification with 'being LGBT' appear to be wider determinants to consider. Other attempts to dismantle the LGBT umbrella term are offered by Mark Simpson, author of 'Anti-Gay' and originator of the term 'metrosexual' (*The Independent*, 1999), and Jack Malebranche's (2007) preferred term for gay male sexuality 'androphilia'. Could it be that while society endeavours to be equal, not only are some less than equal, but those who feel equality has been achieved might 'mutiny' and abandon the LGBT umbrella?

In response to these alternatives, public services should be urged not to consider the term LGBT as prescriptive. It loosely collects a range of identities that may (or may not) give information about an individual's needs. It reminds us that whatever the chosen, adopted or superimposed identity of individuals, the principles of holism (Swinton, 2001) apply now more than ever. Placing the individual at the centre of care and well-being has never been more pertinent. Finally, the Scottish Government recently coined five overarching strategic themes to improve life in Scotland: 'Healthier', 'Wealthier and Fairer', 'Safer and Stronger', 'Smarter' and 'Greener' (Scottish Government, 2008b). Well-being should be central to this, as pertinent to environment, income, learning and safety as it is to health. In order to achieve not only a 'Wealthier' but a 'Healthier' Scotland, it would appear that for LGBT people, public services might also focus on equality as 'Fairness'. Surely this is the key universal theme than can be a 'fit' to 'all'.

CHAPTER 2

'What's He Looking at Me for?' Age, Generation and Categorisation for Gay Men's Health Promotion

Sara MacKian and John E. Goldring

The 'gay community'[1] is very visible in some parts of contemporary society, rooted in a physical territory seen in the manifestation of 'gay villages' or 'gay quarters' across many Western cities. With this in mind the gay community might make an obvious health promotion target for policy makers and those charged with promoting the nation's health. However, by problematising the category 'gay', the notion of 'community' and the significance of gay normative space in the lives of diverse gay men, this chapter questions whether the gay community is an *appropriate* health promotion target.

When you start to contextualise gay men's health, it soon becomes apparent that gay men are 'treated' differently from heterosexual men. This is most evident when exploring differences in health promotion material targeting both populations. When we asked four health promotion units to send us material relating to 'men's health' we were sent a variety of leaflets covering everything from how to look after your heart to testicular cancer, smoking cessation to sexual health, diet and exercise to the changing health needs of men of 40. Ask the same health promotion units for material relating to 'gay men's health', and the difference is stark. In response to this request we received information on HIV/AIDS, sexual health and a small amount on mental health.

While this was not a rigorous exercise designed to assess the understanding of men's health and gay men's health issues across health promotion practice in general, as a simple exercise it demonstrates a very clear message. It is a message that is also reflected in wider health promotion material. To give two examples, the NHS featured a recent campaign targeting women as mothers in their 'Top Tips For Top Mums', and the British Heart Foundation's (BHF) smoking cessation campaign featured over thirty different television adverts targeting a diverse range of audiences with the implicit assumption of heterosexuality, including imagery such as funeral flowers spelling out the words 'dad' and 'mum'. This heteronormative relational context is often drawn upon. On the prostate disease webpage, for example, a grandfather and grandson look out to sea together, and on the BBC Men's Health webpage a father shows his young son how to shave. The front page of Male Health (April 2008) showed a picture of the 'vasec couple' leading to a discussion of 'the facts to consider before having the snip'. This locates visitors to the site clearly within a heterosexual relationship. Even when a campaign makes no explicit reference to the sexual orientation of the main character, we might quite understandably be led to conclude this lack of anything noticeable to link to either a gay or straight identity equates with a lazy assumption of heterosexuality.

The picture of men's health is therefore one underpinned by an implicit heteronormativity. *Men's* identity in this discourse – *and hence their health* – is rooted in lifestyle and life stage, with an emphasis on the individual in a holistic and relational context. *Gay men's* health – *and hence identity* – is predominantly seen in the context of overtly sexual relationships, based on commonly held assumptions about the gay community, or not seen at all. The reality for gay men is that there's more to health than HIV. If gay men face the same health issues as all men, why then are they implicitly and explicitly excluded from health promotion materials and campaigns, or incorporated only in a very narrow fashion?

This chapter explores how we might break down and move beyond the categories of 'gay men' and the 'gay community' in health promotion and policy. Although the emphasis is on gay men, the implications and approach have resonance across any unproblematic categorical delineation of the population and therefore have resonance for lesbian women, bisexuals and trans people also. Empirical findings underpinning the chapter are drawn from two qualitative ethnographic research projects carried out in Manchester in the north-west of England between 2001 and 2007.[2] We draw on the voices of 36 gay participants from these projects, between the ages of 17 and

73 years. Various recruitment strategies were used, with the specific intention of reaching a diverse range of men, including those not easily found in the Gay Village. One of the key findings from the research was the importance of the generational perspectives found within this section of the gay population, and the implication of this for health promotion is the focus of the chapter.

Contextualising gay men's health

It may seem obvious to say there *is* no single gay identity *or* community. Just like heterosexual men, gay men are complex and have complex health needs. But our simple exercise at the start suggests that health promoters treat gay men's and straight men's health differently. There is a limiting discourse surrounding the gay identity pointing to middle-class males who are without need (Keogh *et al.*, 2004), young, hedonistic, most often single and sexually promiscuous (Lee, 2007). It then seems that health promotion considers this narrowly defined stereotypical image of gay men as *the* target audience. Other health needs faced by gay men unconnected to sexual health (HIV especially) are ignored. By implication, health promotion fails to acknowledge other social dimensions known to shape the experience of health.

However, gay men face the same health issues as all men. For example, comparing prevalence of smoking in gay and straight men, rates are higher in gay men (Yamey 2003; Harding, Bensley *et al.*, 2004). Gay men are at particularly high risk of being killed by tobacco, with some evidence suggesting almost half of gay men smoke (Yamey, 2003). Why, then, has this issue not been viewed as a problem within this population, and why have gay men so rarely been made a specific target?

In the Wanless Report (2004) *Securing Good Health for the Whole Population*, it is stressed how communities and sections of communities should be explicitly targeted with appropriate health promotion material and failure to do so may exacerbate health inequalities. The NHS (and health policy generally) have begun to recognise that to promote health requires an understanding of the *context* of peoples' lives (Cayton, 2006). But this is not happening for gay men, who face a triple whammy: their health is limited to 'sexual health', they are perceived in a narrow stereotypical manner, and they are missing from mainstream health promotion material.

So we have to look at the specific circumstances gay men find themselves in, to make it context-specific. We do that by looking at the flourishing social settings gay men have access to – in this case in Manchester's Gay Village – as well as the changing social and cultural climate they experience.

Contextualising the data

It is worth thinking about just how much things have changed for gay men in England,[3] from what was once a quite authoritarian regime before the decriminalisation of homosexuality in 1967 to the equalisation of sexual consent in 2001. Pre-1967, homosexuality was illegal and punishable by imprisonment. In 1967 homosexuality was decriminalised but only for those over 21 and strictly in private. No such restrictions existed for heterosexual sexual relations.[4] In 1994 the age of consent was reduced to 18 receiving a considerable amount of negative media coverage. Post-2001 we entered a more egalitarian climate with the equalisation of age of consent.

Such tremendous legal changes are bound to affect the social and cultural experiences of gay men. They have also had a profound effect on gay social scenes. To the casual observer, the contemporary emergence of the gay identity across space in the form of gay villages from Manchester to Manhattan, Sydney to Stockholm may seem an exclusively positive development, as many generations of gay men grew up without such safe places to meet openly with other gay men. Our generational exploration however suggests a more nuanced understanding of the current role of gay normative space. By exploring how the physical context of gay men's experiences has changed in Manchester we start to see the relevance of breaking down simplistic categories if we are truly to move beyond arbitrary markers of identity, such as gay, to the genuine situated experiences of individuals. The physical context is an important place to start as it houses, influences and provides the stage for the performance of everyday identity.

The physical presence of gay communities in Manchester has altered enormously. Prior to the decriminalisation of homosexuality, the gay experience was pushed underground because of the authoritarian treatment of gay men by the state. As George (aged 73) told us, 'It would be difficult for anyone who did not live through those times to understand.' The degree of symbolic violence inflicted on gay men was both real and experienced. Another of our participants, 72-year-old Jack was imprisoned 'by association' for 6 months 'hard labour', simply because his name and address were found on a man caught having sex with another man. This very real threat led most gay man to conceal their identity, making gay space invisible, even to other men in the same situation. As Thomas (aged 72), told us, he did not know there were other men like him in the world, until he was introduced to the underground gay scene in Manchester. Even after the 1967 decriminalisation of homosexuality, gay men were still driven underground, metaphorically and literally. As part of the changing social climate, more gay normative space, by which we mean a social setting where being gay is the norm, emerged in Manchester in what is now known as the Gay Village, but even post-1967 known gay venues were routinely raided by the police and clubs were frequently closed down.

By the 1990s the gay 'scene' had arrived and located itself visibly in the urban fabric of most Western cities. In Manchester, visible markers of gay confidence grew with the development of the Gay Village as bars and clubs rose from the cellars and archways following major gentrification begun along sections of the Rochdale canal in the 1990s (Skeggs, 1999). Nowadays being a young gay man is very different from the experiences of George, Thomas and Jack. For a younger gay man growing up today there is a vibrant gay scene found in many major cities and issues around sexual diversity are reflected in popular culture with television shows such as *Queer as Folk* as well as in more mainstream programming such as *Coronation Street, EastEnders* and even *Grange Hill.* With this cultural and social shift has come greater integration, and the emergence of a mixed door policy in most of the venues in the Village in Manchester, allowing entry to both men and women, gay and non-gay.

However, this changing context will not be experienced in the same way by all gay men. There are considerably diverse experiences and one set of differences emerged clearly in the data around age and generation. We now propose to explore these generational differences found in the research, before moving on to discuss the implications of this for health promotion, for individuals and for health policy more generally.

The inter-generational framework

The historical context that shaped the social and legal climate we see today led us to approach the data using an inter-generational framework based around the three legal changes since the 1967 decriminalisation of homosexuality in England (Table 2.1).

Reflecting the concern that existing health promotion material either ignores gay men or targets one narrow section, we wish to focus on differences in attitude across these generations to gay normative space, and the implications this might have for health promotion campaigns that specifically use that space and scene as a central motif. The following sections therefore draw on the words of respondents to illustrate the changing experience of gay normative space across the generations.

Table 2.1: The generational framework

Generation	Legal change	Gay career	Age at interview
'Criminal'	Pre-1967 Homosexuality illegal	Could begin their gay career whilst homosexuality was still illegal	55 years plus
'Legal 21'	1967 Sexual Offences Bill – age of consent set at 21	Could begin their gay career after the decriminalisation of homosexuality but before the age of consent was reduced	31-54 years
'Legal 18'	1994 Criminal Justice and Public Order Act – age of consent reduced to 18	Could begin their gay career between 1994 and 2001 when the age of consent was reduced from 21 to 18	22-30 years
'Legal 16'	2001 age of consent reduced to 16	Could begin their gay career post-2001 when the age of consent was equalised	16-21 years

The Criminal Generation: a continued role for 'community'

Much recent academic work has charted the growth of gay spaces in urban areas as indicative of both gay men and women's capacity for appropriating space in a heteronormative society, and as a reflection of an increasing acceptance of 'homosexuality' in the spaces of the city (see for example Hindle, 2001). For the early part of their lives, men in the Criminal Generation had experienced their marginality without the ready availability of such gay normative space. Many had fought for and won such space and could still recall what life was like in its absence: 'If it wasn't there … it would be [like it was] when I was a young man … isolation … you would have to hide your sexuality' (Jack, 72 years).

The Criminal Generation held optimistic attitudes towards the idea of the gay community and continued to link the use of gay space to their sense of community/identity. Several participants in this generation had moved to Manchester specifically to be a part of what was considered a vibrant gay community.

A wealth of research charts the demise of such spaces due to the 'degaying' of places like Manchester's Gay Village with the influx of ever-growing numbers of heterosexual visitors using the space both as a safe enclave and as a place of spectacle (see for example Binnie and Skeggs, 2004; Ellis, 2007). Those in the Criminal Generation had witnessed this and they began to recognise limitations of the Village, feeling it was no longer as safe as it had been.

Legal 21: ambivalence of gay space – no man's land

This sense of demise (or community lost) was reflected most strongly in the Legal 21 Generation, for whom the sense of place that once came with the

Gay Village had been supplanted with experiences of intolerance and lack of understanding about the norms and values of gay people. For instance, the paradox of integration and trespass were profoundly experienced:

> I am for integration … but, to a certain extent it can be counterproductive when you think that … gay people going into straight bars, [and] the straight men cause the trouble because they think 'what's he looking at me for?' it's a safer environment for gay people to have their own areas. (Chris, 34 years)

So Chris would like integration in theory, but such negative experiences had not only turned him away from using many venues in the Gay Village, but to some degree, turned him against it. Similarly Nick had an ambivalent relationship with the Village:

> I really do object to this, well there was one guy in The Rembrandt, he was straight and he was complaining to his girlfriend that someone was fucking looking at him. And I thought, well yes, in a fucking gay pub, if you don't like it, fuck off! (Nick, 41 years)

For the Legal 21 Generation, there was a cynicism towards the Village and the scene – both key visible markers of the gay community. Many in this cohort continued to use the Gay Village socially, but begrudgingly.

Legal 18: rejection of gay space

All but one of the Legal 18 Generation had grown out of gay space and had moved on in what appeared to be a 'settling down' process. In the past, many had used the gay scene extensively but increasingly it seemed it did not keep pace with them; they had changed, the scene had not:

> Four or five years ago I was obsessed … everything had to be gay. My hair had to be cut by a gay hairdresser. I had to see a gay doctor. I had to drink in gay bars. I had to go to the toilet in gay toilets. That's how gay I was. But I've just grown out of that. It has no interest to me at all. (Ryan, 22 years)

Many in this generation had stopped using the Gay Village regularly and only saw it as a means to an end as a place to meet other gay men. Even David, the one participant in this cohort who still had some psychological sense of belonging to the Gay Village, was very particular about the venues he used having a 'men only' door policy. When asked why, he suggested it was because they had the kind of people he wanted to associate with:

[the] gay people that I can get on with and don't grind on me because of forced campness and don't look down on me because I'm not a seven stone weakling like all the twinks in Essential. (David, 23 years)

Again, gay space was not viewed positively and it was ultimately rejected. However, echoing the previous two generations, there seemed little sense of integrating into heteronormative space as we see for the next generation.

Legal 16: your place or mine?

The men in the Legal 16 Generation were more integrated with straight/mixed social networks than any other generation. They also separated the gay scene from the gay community quite markedly and had a more experiential interpretation of what community was for them:

> When I say gay community, I think people being friends, sex not ever coming into it. It's a bunch of gay guys just being friends, and that's the gay community. When I hear 'gay scene', [I] think ... condoms, lube and toilets ... I prefer community to scene, there is a difference in my mind. (Jacob, 21 years)

In part this was a reflection of the fact that many had a negative image of gay normative space and the people that used it. Josh explains that he will socialise with his friends rather than in a particular space:

> Wherever my friends are going really. We go to [straight bars] ... I tend to go with friends and sort of stay with them when I'm in the Village. A lot of people there are a bit shallow and not the sort of people I like to talk to really. (Josh, 18 years)

This generation disliked the highly sexualised nature of the gay scene and the physical gay community's association with the scene made it a less desirable space in their experience.

Discussion

In summary then, with the changing social and legal climate have come changing attitudes towards gay space among gay men, with differences reflected across the generations. Despite the apparent increased opportunities for gay men to openly explore and experience their sexuality in gay normative spaces, such physical manifestations of space for the gay population have not come without some attendant problems. This has been widely documented in the literature already (see for example Binnie and Skeggs, 2004; Ellis, 2007).

However what we are suggesting is that there are particular experiences based around generational categories that might be usefully explored further in order to enhance our situated understanding of health promotion in relation to gay men. Without wanting to overly complicate the discussion, it is worth locating this theoretically, as there are concepts from social science we can utilise to develop a more nuanced understanding of gay experiences, an understanding that could point the way towards more effective and appropriate health promotion activities.

The social and legal changes in the gay experience, and the way in which men talked about and adjusted to them, led us to locate our data in the theoretical framework developed around 'reflexive individualisation' (see for example Beck, 1994; Giddens, 1991). The general suggestion, in what Adams (2003) has described as 'the extended reflexivity thesis', is that key familiar institutions that underpinned modernisation – such as the family, the Welfare State, the job for life – have given way to a less certain world, to an infinite variety of identities and potentialities, limited only by our own imagination and nerve. In this context the individual no longer has comfortable taken-for-granted structures to identify with and locate themselves within. The 'reflexive individual' therefore has to cobble together their own DIY identities and networks, to create new meaningful existences for themselves.

Contrary to what some people have suggested (see for example Furedi, 2007), this does not necessarily mean atomization, isolation and loneliness – Margaret Thatcher's end of society – but instead the 'disembedding and re-embedding' of ways of being and doing as people 'cobble together' their biographies (Beck, 1994, p. 13). Reflexive individualisation as a theory has met with much criticism. For example it has been highlighted as being elitist and exclusionary, applicable only to certain sections of the population, and it ignores wider structural barriers to reflexive actualisation such as gender or ethnicity (see for example Skeggs, 2004). While we accept the limitations of the theoretical framework, and acknowledge the fact that reflexive individualisation is not positive for all sections of society, we feel in many ways this process has benefited gay men by giving them the freedoms from which to construct their identity, relationships and network associations. It is therefore useful to draw upon in the context of this paper.

For gay men the breaking down of traditional institutions has facilitated the weakening of some of the exclusionary mechanisms that had long served to mediate their social, cultural and legal experiences, and allowed a greater range of legitimate social and spatial claims to be made. Gay men can now come out in relative safety and are able to locate themselves physically in spaces like Manchester's Gay Village. An increasingly reflexive society has enabled the development and partial acceptance of such things as civil partnerships, gay adoption and other markers of visibility (as outlined in Chapter 1). However with this individualisation process came a kind of skewed integration. The rest of society has *also* opened up reflexively, women on hen nights can now choose to party in the gay village where they will feel distanced from the sexually predatory activities of heterosexual men, for example. There has therefore been a loss of gay normative space with implications for how gay men relate to and use it; it quite simply is no longer positively viewed as gay space and it does not belong to the gay community or the gay population more generally. The blurring of the boundaries between gay and straight seems very much a one-way transaction and despite the category 'gay' becoming more flexible and accepted within wider society, the prevailing sense was that being gay in a heteronormative space carries potential risks. The loss of gay spaces means that gay men no longer have the safe social settings to enact their normative behaviours away from the heterosexual gaze. Moreover, the disenchantment felt by gay men towards the gay community effectively deprives health promoters of their captive audience at whom they can target health messages.

Conclusions: implications of age and generation

So far we have explored the changing legal and social climate gay men find themselves negotiating in the city of Manchester, England. We have suggested that going beyond the simplistic category of the 'gay community' reveals a complex experiential picture that cannot be captured with such loose labels. We have shown a diversity of gay experience, in this instance, structured by individual biography and historical context. Although the focus here has been on gay men, it is no hard task to see that such differences exist for all, regardless of sexual orientation. The point we are emphasizing is that this simple detail has not been recognized and acknowledged within health policy or reflected in health promotion material. So what then are the implications of failing to recognize this complexity within apparently homogenous categories such as 'gay men'? We identify three broad areas of concerns: implications for health promotion, implications for individuals, and finally implications for policy.

Implications for health promotion

We will begin where we started, with health promotion materials. Health promotion campaigns are, on the whole, predicated on two basic assumptions: health is influenced by behaviour, and behaviour is modifiable (Conner and Norman 1996). The downfall of this sometimes is the assumption that the individual is a detached rational decision maker, systematically reviewing available information and forming behaviour intentions from this. This loses the sense that we are all rooted in social contexts that affect, in far more complex ways, how we process and act on information (see for example MacKian, Bedri *et al.*, 2004). While health promotion materials are becoming more sophisticated in a UK context, there is still a long way to go. One particular failure has been the apparent inability to provide sufficiently diverse material to appeal to anything other than a narrow range of very stereotypical types – the 'family man', the 'concerned mother', the 'young gay twink'.

There might be many reasons why heterosexual men miss health promotion messages, but what we are suggesting in this chapter is that there are three key reasons *gay men specifically* might miss important health promotion messages. Firstly, as we have demonstrated, there is an absence of meaningful imagery when communicating 'mainstream' men's health promotion materials. Secondly, we can add to this the implicit linking of the gay identity with HIV and AIDS to the omission of all other relevant health messages. Where material is specifically targeted towards gay men, this is predominantly situated within the HIV discourse. Thirdly, even if we are to begin to communicate with gay men in health messages, we must not assume that all gay men will positively identify with the gay community. Much 'gay' targeted material draws on the central motif of the gay community, which invariably is knowingly or unknowingly equated with 'the scene'. The hidden majority of gay men simply do not relate to, identify with, or frequent these spaces. Taking these three considerations together, we start to see why some gay men could be missing important health messages.

There appear to be two processes at work. Firstly, there is an element of *self-defined marginality* with men distancing themselves from the gay community. Many men quite simply do not identify with it. The visible expression of gay community has become dominated by the gay scene and this alienates some generations and many individuals as it has no currency in their lives. We can see here how the processes of 'reflexive individualisation' have both constrained gay men's experiences, through the de-gaying of gay normative space, and facilitated their ability to construct alternative identities not rooted in the visible gay scene – particularly as witnessed with the youngest generation.

Secondly there is a marked degree of *symbolic marginality* on the part of health practice approaches. The convenience of targeting the 'gay community' demonstrates a willingness to engage with diversity. However, it is a rather cursory engagement, and assuming a homogenised gay community may turn away those who do not identify with it. We see here how the reflexive opening up of society has allowed recognition of gay men in health discourse. However, the way in which this is incorporated is very *non*-reflexive. There is little problematisation of what gay community *as an experience* means for what is after all an extremely varied population. In loose catch-all phrases like the 'gay community' health promoters may therefore unwittingly turn away those who do not identify with it and quite simply never even reach those who are not active on the scene.

Such double marginalisation is concerning given that gay men demonstrate considerable health competency in some areas, in part a reflection of having to manage their well-being and health alongside the threat of HIV/AIDS (see Bellaby *et al.*, 2007). We now turn therefore to individual implications of gay men's marginalisation from health promotion.

Implications for individuals
Anybody may be at risk of missing the point of, or missing entirely, a particular health promotion message, regardless of their sexual orientation. What we are suggesting is that applying a narrow definition of gay is a limiting enterprise that has the potential of missing many of the intended targets. In so doing, there are very real implications for individual health, and to illustrate this we offer three simple vignettes drawn from the legal 21 generation. Each man, with his own story, illustrates the implications for individuals of failing to take on board important health messages (see Table 2.2).

Clearly any health policy needs to draw on categories to some extent to simplify the task at hand, identify likely targets and develop some guidelines for working with particular populations. However, we feel that the category 'gay' has to some extent blinded health promotion and if understood in a more nuanced way such categories could serve to support health promotion aims rather than undermine them. Thus while it might be the case that these health promotion campaigns have not worked for all sections of the heterosexual population either, gay men offer a particularly interesting case for the following

Table 2.2: Individual implications

Categorisation becomes stereotyping...	Categorisation serves to hide health messages...	When categories become unpredictable...
Chris, 35 years, was exposed to the HIV virus when his partner's condom split. He was unaware of PEP (Post Exposure Prophylaxis), which can prevent HIV taking hold. When he did go out in the village he had seen safer sex posters but not posters advertising PEP. He did not read much of the free gay press as he considered it to be targeted at the younger 'twinky' gay man, which in his words 'didn't mean me'. Had he done, he might have known about PEP and may not now be HIV positive. The stereotype of the gay man does not resonate with Chris due to his body size and age.	Grant, 38 years, falls into the most obvious category of 'gay man', being relatively affluent, single, middle class and educated. By focusing on his gay identity health promoters have successfully reached Grant who has a vast knowledge and understanding about safer-sex practices. However, as a committed celibate who has never embarked on a sexual relationship, HIV is one health issue he need not have on his radar. If health promoters took a broader view of the category 'gay' they would see how other health issues require addressing. For instance, Grant had low awareness around 'healthy hearts' despite having a very unhealthy diet and binge-drinking three or four nights a week.	Martin, 42 years, has been in what appears to be a heterosexual relationship for the last two decades and lives 20 miles outside Manchester. He has known about his sexual orientation since a teenager and has been sexually active since. He first heard reports of AIDS in the early 1980s when in the Merchant Navy, 'bonking his way around the world'. He felt it did not concern him, as it was some exotic disease from Africa that affected Africans. So he and everybody else he knew, 'kind of ignored it'. Now some 20 years on, Martin knows a lot more about HIV and AIDS. His lifestyle makes it difficult to get down to the Gay Village. 'Like being a part time gay', his only contact with gay men is via cruising grounds and gay saunas. He feels lucky living in the 'sticks' as 'you don't get high incidence of HIV'. Martin is still ignoring it and despite him not knowing his current HIV status, he does not use a condom.

reasons. Firstly, all our participants could demonstrate a vast understanding of safer sex and HIV prevention and therefore some level of 'health competency'. This was largely down to the very *successful* use of categorisation to target gay men as a population during HIV/AIDS advertising in recent decades. Secondly, however, this 'skill' was not transferred to the understanding of other health promotions.

Implications for policy

If we return, finally, to where we started, with the simple exercise of collecting health promotion material, it is indicative that despite a considerably more favourable climate for gay men legally and socially, there is still a way to go to ensure stereotyping does not restrict the way in which health messages are produced and communicated. It is not acceptable for health promotion material or health professionals to assume unproblematic identities, and it is vital that the discourse moves beyond the simplistic gay–straight dichotomy. More tailored health messages are both respectful and potentially more effective.

The famous gay pride slogan stated 'We are all equal'. However, it is time to recognise within health policy and practice, that while we may all be equal, we are *not* all the same. Failure to recognise this, as Wanless (2004) suggested, can exacerbate inequalities. The evidence presented in this chapter suggests that it is high time we question the use of the 'gay community' as a concept at all and start to develop policies, practices and discourses that reflect the reality of situated experience.

Notes

1. We put this phrase in inverted commas in this introductory sentence to reflect the way in which it has emerged in popular and academic discourse as an unproblematised and commonly understood phenomenon and concept; also to reflect our dis-ease with this widespread non-reflexive application.

2. The first study was funded by an NHS Fellowship and the second by an ESRC Small Grant.

3. The laws decriminalising homosexuality were not unified across the United Kingdom. In Scotland it was 1980 and in Northern Ireland, 1982.

4. This anomaly did not change until 2004 when the Sexual Offences Act of 2003 deleted gross indecency and buggery from statute.5.

CHAPTER 3

A Path Less Travelled: Hearing the Voices of Older Lesbians

Carole Archibald

(Wo)man cannot discover new oceans until (s)he has courage to lose sight of the shore. *(Unknown)*

Introduction

The above metaphor of travel and journeying is apt for me in terms of the study described in this chapter. I undertook this research following my doctoral degree (PhD), which looked at the sexual expression of people with dementia in residential care. Often people undertake research as part of career progression. In my late fifties I was more motivated by one of the findings of my PhD (Archibald, 2002) that pointed to considerable discrimination showed by some women care workers towards an elderly resident with mental health problems and some cognitive impairment, perceived to be a lesbian.

As in any residential home situation, labels and identities, and specifically that of lesbian identity, were here part of a complex web of interactions, including my own. I wanted to explore these issues further with a view to informing practice, and possibly going on to undertake a larger study. It was a worthy idea, if somewhat naïve, that my identity as a woman would be sufficient to set me on the road to meeting with and exploring issues with older lesbians. The recruitment of respondents proved far more difficult and time-consuming than anticipated. Sexual identities are one of the main themes of this book and in undertaking this pilot it quickly became apparent that the sexual identity of the researcher could be an issue. This is something I return to later in this chapter. But as I proceeded, it became obvious that it was a path less travelled, not only by mainstream research but also by feminist researchers, whatever their sexual orientation.

Feminism has, as its core, the emancipatory and validating notion of providing a voice for women. While there are a number of gerontologists working within a feminist framework, for example Arber, Davidson and Ginn (2003), Ray (2004), and Whittaker (1995), feminist scholarship in general has paid little attention to later life. There also appears to be a gap in feminist debate concerning how women themselves may be instrumental in the oppression of other women, as is discussed in the work of Bernard (1998), Evers (1981) and Lee-Treweek (1994).

Relevant literature

With some exceptions, e.g. Cronin (2004), Hubbard and Rossington (1995), Lee (2005, 2007) and Price (2005, 2008), the research community in the UK has largely ignored LGBT older people, with no research involving any sizeable samples of older lesbians and gay men before 2001 (Turnbull, 2001). Two years on, Heaphy *et al.* (2003) addressed this gap by recruiting a larger research sample (n= 266) but the invisibility of older lesbians is apparent, with just under 40% of this sample being women and, of these, 78% were in their 50s.

There are a number of reasons for this lack of research interest, including heterosexism within social gerontology (Cronin, 2004), resulting in older lesbians being overlooked and not catered for, but there are other components involved. There is a real tension between the need to challenge homophobia and heterosexist attitudes by undertaking research and hearing the voices of people who are often marginalised, and the 'danger' that exists for them as participants in that research. Keeping hidden and 'passing' has long been a strategy and a coping mechanism in such areas as health care for older people where homophobia is reported to be more prevalent (Brotman *et al.*, 2003) and where research access is often limited to those active within lesbian and gay communities (Friend, 1990). Such tensions in research have obvious parallels with the challenges present in practice settings and the provision of services and support to older lesbian women.

One dilemma is the question of how to tailor services to individuals who are uncertain about disclosing their sexuality to service providers. Decisions over disclosure or 'coming out' are often influenced by perceptions of an agency or service. Settings that openly recognise sexual diversity are more likely to be accessed by LGB users, who in turn will feel more secure in disclosing their sexuality (further discussed by Cronin and King in Chapter 6). In other words, it is helpful for providers to think of the coming out process as a dynamic in which their own approach and ethos play a significant role.

While 'passing' and being closeted and therefore not so easily identified as LGB can be of issue (Heaphy *et al.*, 2003; Brotman *et al.*, 2003), all too often this 'invisibility' masks a lack of effort made by researchers and service providers alike to engage with specific minority groups, particularly older lesbians. This has resulted in research into the long-stay care needs of this group of women being virtually non-existent. Without such research it is difficult to imagine how evidence-based practice will develop in this area.

Working with older LGBT people

Despite the shortage of research and policy focusing on older LGBT people, the voluntary sector in the UK has provided the lead in developing work around sexuality and ageing. As is often the case with such targeted work, much of this activity can be characterised as time-limited, one-off initiatives with finite funding. Mainstream service providers have so far proved slow to take up this work and develop more lasting patterns of provision, or to engage older LGBT individuals in discussions over their experiences and perspectives on existing services.

Much work within the voluntary sector has been participative in design and shaped by close consultation and involvement of older LGBT individuals. The Age Concern Opening Doors programme has helped to co-ordinate working in this area and provides specific resources for service planners and providers (see www.ageconcern.org.uk/openingdoors). This includes a recent guide to good practice in care home settings (Knocker, 2006). Projects involving older lesbians and gay men have been undertaken in a number of areas, including an investigation into the social care needs of older gay men and lesbians in Merseyside (Kitchen, 2003). Polari in London and Gay and Grey in Dorset have each undertaken participative projects, which are compared and discussed in Ward, River and Fenge (2008). Both these initiatives were intended to serve as prototypes that might be taken up and adapted by groups and agencies in other areas. Polari has also undertaken a scoping study of the needs of older lesbians in central London (River, 2006). Working with the support of the Alzheimer's Society a number of volunteers have developed a lesbian, gay, bisexual and transgender support group providing telephone support to those affected by dementia across the UK.

To date, and with the exception of this study and an investigation into housing needs and options (Communities Scotland, 2005), there remains very little research into the needs and experiences of older LGBT people in Scotland. And, despite a clear commitment to engaging with and recognising the needs and interests of LGBT groups and individuals (e.g. through the Hearts and Minds agenda) the Scottish Government has largely overlooked the older generations within these communities. It is here that we see how intersecting identities can lead to patterns of exclusion. To be an older lesbian woman means being vulnerable to multiple forms of discrimination, as so forcefully described from a personal perspective by the likes of Barbara Macdonald (1983) and Baba Copper (1988).

Turnbull (2001) notes that in the mainly North American literature there appears to be a vibrant research culture; however, the research is biased towards those living in large urban areas, with research participants mainly white and better educated, and tends not to differentiate between gay men and women. This bias mirrors the situation in the UK with little or no research or development work specifically targeting those in rural settings or from black and minority ethnic groups. To date there is also a clear emphasis on gay men and lesbians with far less work undertaken with older bisexual or trans individuals.

The broader range of LGBT work that does exist has undoubtedly contributed to the acknowledgement of LGBT issues/identities by the public sector with the development in health and social care of equalities policies. However, it remains to be seen how well services to older people will cater for sexual diversity in later life given that sexuality in general is often such a problematic issue in this area of provision (Archibald, 2002; Ward *et al.*, 2005). Recent evidence suggests that in care practice the categories of 'old' and 'lesbian' are often viewed as incompatible (River, 2006).

My pilot study, started in 2002, adds to the body of information available and is unique in exploring lesbian perspectives on long-term care in a Scottish context.

The Pilot Study

Whereas Heaphy *et al.* (2003) were readily able to recruit many women in their middle years, older lesbians were another matter and this has been true of my pilot study despite undertaking this research in mainly urban areas of Scotland. 'Older' in my study therefore has come to be defined as women aged around 60 years old, women about my own age.

Identities

As a feminist I consider that an important part of the research process should entail the researcher being reflexive so that she/he does not divide parts of the (researcher's) self from the whole (Rose and Webb, 1998, p. 556). It is necessary therefore to analyse the effect of (my)self within the research process as I am, as Webb (1992) notes, an integral aspect of the generation of knowledge and this will inevitably shape and determine what I 'see'.

A middle-aged, white, middle-class heterosexual woman, I came to this research ignorant of many of the very real difficulties that older and younger lesbians sometimes encounter simply because of their sexual orientation. This research therefore included challenging my own heterosexist attitudes evident in retrospect when I was a health visitor and undertaking my doctoral research, and homophobia. The latter, as Metz (1997) notes, affects all people to some degree however liberal.

The difficulty in recruiting a research sample caused me to question whether my sexual identity placed me at a disadvantage. One woman who was not part of the research sample but who spoke at length on the phone confirmed these growing concerns. When I gave a résumé of what the study was about and the difficulty in recruiting a sample this woman's immediate question was 'Are you gay?' and when I replied in the negative her response was: 'That explains it! You are working with one hand tied behind your back'.

It was a rather dispiriting start and begged the question of whether being a lesbian was a prerequisite to undertake research in this area or whether our shared membership of the category 'woman' would be sufficient to build the contacts and trust needed to recruit respondents. In terms of gaining access, it might have been easier for potential respondents to trust what I was going to do with their words if I had myself been lesbian (for example, see Ward, Jones *et al.*, 2008, who used approximately 'matched' researchers and interviewees and had less difficulty recruiting respondents). But I think there is a case to be made that my being an 'outsider' meant that interviewees had to explain things in more detail than if they had perceived me as an insider.

The women I worked with in the study

In total, the sample comprised five 'older' women and further information was obtained by an interview with a social work manager of a residential home who was lesbian and in her thirties.

To obtain sufficient numbers of participants, I used snowballing, that is contacting one participant and asking if she knew anyone else who would be prepared to talk to me, then asking the next participant the same question until I finally obtained a suitable sample. The whole process was difficult and time consuming, taking months to recruit this small sample. Whether being a lesbian and thus better networked would have helped is worth consideration. However, having colleagues who are gay and who could vouch for me was in the end the most important way of gaining access.

In the rest of this chapter I discuss the findings from my study, focusing particularly on the ways in which participants did and did not use the identity label 'older lesbian'.

Demographic background information

Table 3.1 provides an aggregate of the age, education and the work of the five older women involved. Friend (1990) and others note that often recruiting participants is limited to those active within their communities. Of the five women interviewed, three are actively involved in the lesbian community with the others leading their lives as a couple, not going out much but remaining socially involved with some friends. These latter women reported going to the cinema or being involved in a walking group in terms of leisure activities.

Table 3.1: Participant profiles

Age	58 -73 (mean age 62 years)
Education	2 went to university, 3 left school between 15-17years
Relationships	3 divorced, all of whom have children, 2 women are single and have never married or had children. Of the 5, 2 have partners, 1 has a partner intermittently
Employment	Ranges from teaching/secretarial/nursing/political involvement, 2 women now retired though remain activists

One woman reported she was in her own comfort zone with gay friends and, mainly, participants reported that their friends are gay, saying for example: 'I have a good circle of friends who are mainly gay, and that is enough for me'.

A finding that resonates with the literature both in the US (Beeler *et al.*, 1999) and the UK (Heaphy and Yip, 2003; Ward, Jones *et al.*, 2008) is that ageism is apparent on the gay and lesbian scene in the main Scottish cities 'where social life tends to revolve around youthful clubbing and pubbing' which is, one participant reported, 'rather predatory – looking for younger women'.

Several of the women interviewed have partners but for those that do not it can be difficult as they get older as sexual needs remain. As one participant noted: 'There is little chance of a partner now yet I still have need for a sexual life.'

With most of the five women, their partner or their 'family of choice' (Donovan, Heaphy and Weeks, 2001) appears to assume most importance with several reporting sometimes severe difficulties and discrimination from their family of origin. Those who were married with children report that mainly their children have been accepting, and one woman reported that when she told her children about her sexual orientation, one of them felt that they were then able to 'come out' about their own gay sexuality.

Coming out

Decisions concerning 'coming out', as noted earlier, can be associated with issues around discrimination but equally and importantly they can relate to people's sense of identity. Coming out is about coming into ownership of an identity category with its attendant benefits and disadvantages. For some, coming out is seen as authenticity and the acceptance of the true self, while remaining closeted is an act of dishonesty. Rosenfeld (1999) notes that it is the elder gay liberationists who are lionised by younger generations, like war heroes, with those not out given little political or cultural recognition.

'Out-ness' is a complex, very personal issue. Some health professionals may still consider homosexuality a mental disorder (Brotman *et al.*, 2003) so trusting professionals who represent these organisations does not come easily (Cohen *et al.*, 2008).

Being 'out' therefore can have major implications with regard to its impact in health and care settings. Studies that describe lesbian experiences of health services point to these tending, on the whole, to be negative but this seemed to depend on who you are out to. Many in the studies were not old and frail yet encounters with health professionals appear to reflect a good deal of anxiety and strategising (Aronson, 1998). Questions asked by health professionals assumed that they were heterosexual, that their partners were men and that they had roles as mothers or wives, with no routine comfortable way to inform health care providers otherwise (Brotman *et al.*, 2003).

It is evident from both the literature and this data that coming out is not a once and for all situation and requires a degree of courage. There are subtleties involved and often it depends on a number of factors such as whether people are out or not, with whom, and when this occurs. One woman in my pilot study, while being out to her friends, did not come out to her children until they had all left school, as she reported that she did not want her children to be ridiculed. Another reported that she was out when her children were younger and that 'the children in a way suffered, that is the bit you would like to undo'.

For two of the women interviewed who worked either as teachers or in the caring professions, retirement was the time when they could be fully out without prejudicing or compromising themselves. Prior to that, those in teaching reported that fear of losing their jobs caused them to be very discreet about whom they told. One of these women reported:

> Yes, I think that's ... when I was teaching it was before all the furore about paedophilia but I'm sure it was the case that out gay people wouldn't have been given jobs as teachers in the middle 70s. It would have been an assumption that you were automatically an unsuitable person to be teaching.

'Unsuitable' in that context implied the corrupting influence of being a lesbian. The association of being gay with paedophilia was mentioned by the first two women I interviewed so this was added to the interview schedule for the remainder of interviewees. All reported being very aware of the paedophilia association and reported that they or gay people they knew avoided placing themselves in a position where this type of accusation might be levelled at them: 'We are very cautious with other people's children, not over stepping. We never have the neighbour's children in here because you never know.'

The social work manager interviewed has been out since her late 20s and she reports that she is going to be out for the rest of her life. She feels that if she was a resident in a care home and asked about her life history she would miss out on whole chunks of her life if she could not acknowledge she was a lesbian. With such a small sample it is impossible to be sure whether this reflects a broader generational difference. Manthorpe and Price (2003) make the point that many activists involved in the gay liberation movement of the late 60s and early 70s are now reaching later life and may well have very different expect-ations of care services. How well prepared are services to older people for an influx of service users who have been out for most of their lives?

Most of the women interviewed for this study wanted to be discreet about who they came out to. A lot of what was said seemed to be about being accepted not standing out and about others getting to know them first as women/people rather than seeing them first and foremost as gay: 'In your 20s you just want to be accepted – nobody wants to be different everyone wants to be like everyone else.'

The idea of seeing lesbians as essentially ordinary women rather than some exotic species was considered important to most interviewed.

Getting older and lesbian identity

There were a number of women who disliked the term 'lesbian' preferring the word gay, which again perhaps reflected a generational difference from younger lesbian women:

> It is only in recent years I have been using it (lesbian) and I don't know why I find it so unpleasant as a word it just doesn't have a nice ring to it – strange. I started using it because years ago people started using gay and that encompassed both men and women. I believe that there was an actual policy for women to get the word lesbian used so that they were distinguished from men and not all lumped together.

> For a long time I didn't call myself lesbian because of the association with pornography I just saw myself as a gay woman or homosexual preferably.

> I think of myself first as a person before I'm a lesbian. If a person said give one word to describe you 'lesbian' would not be the word I would think about.

For one of the women being lesbian defined who she was but others saw themselves as a woman first with sexual identity being part of who they are. This finding underscores the multiple identities that these women subscribe to and the multiple roles they play in their day-to-day lives.

Such comments also begged the question that, if women do not want to describe themselves as 'lesbian', is it the case that health and social care professionals need to be aware of and use a repertoire of different identity categories? If the woman is out do they need to ask how she would like to be identified? Such individual variance points to the importance of taking a person-centred approach to offering care and support.

Becoming older as a lesbian was seen in a positive light ('I love being my age') in that these women reported being more confident and at 'ease in their skin' about being lesbians. One participant talked about the joy of being involved in Gay Pride marches whereas others reported that these public displays were useful to a point but they also helped to reinforce stereotypes. One woman reported that becoming older meant she became more (sexually) invisible which in a way made life easier. But none of the women interviewed considered themselves old and in need of services. They had had few experiences with social or health services but when they had, their experiences paralleled those noted in the literature (Cohen *et al.*, 2008).

Experiences of social or health care services

For this group, their experiences of health contact tended to be around having a cervical smear or, in one case, breast cancer. The assumption of heterosexuality that underpinned staff questioning and the ensuing embarrassment when they discovered the woman was a lesbian were noted:

> Recently I visited my GP. She looked at my notes [where it was noted that she was a lesbian from a previous health-screening visit] and was obviously very embarrassed. 'I don't think we need to do a smear' she said. I don't know whether she thought I was going to have an orgasm …

The respondent was highly amused at the discomfiture of the GP, hence the funny remark, but it does point up that the GP's response would, for someone less worldly wise, result in health education messages not getting across. Most of the women interviewed reported that they would be wary of coming out to some professionals, echoing the findings of Brotman *et al.* (2003) and Beeler *et al.* (1999) in North America and River (2006) in the UK.

What these women want from health and social services as they get older

As these women are mainly 'third-agers' and do not inhabit the category 'older lesbian', this raised some problems for my research. In an attempt to address this, I asked the five women interviewed to assume an older lesbian identity and think about what would be important to them if they were to be admitted to long-term care or needed community services. A number of issues emerged including the gender identity of staff. Two of the women interviewed wanted to be cared for by women carers.

> The most important, top priority would be for intimate bodily care … I would absolutely demand, would make a great fuss for care like this to be given by female staff.

The social work manager I interviewed reported that some female care staff have difficulty in providing care to lesbians, a finding echoed in my PhD. When I discussed this with the other participants in the pilot study they made the point that the obvious need was for staff training on these issues. One woman noted that being a lesbian does not mean that they are out to seduce all female staff:

> It is important to get across in a lot of people's heads that although I love one woman that is my partner, it doesn't mean I want to love all women … so that they don't feel threatened by it. Try to get people to understand that it's okay I'm not going to attack you because you are a woman.

It is apparent when looking at the literature that there has often been a collective failure to provide education and training on older lesbian and gay issues for staff working in both health and social work (Berkman and Zinberg, 1997; Byron Smith, 1993). Metz (1997) provides an excellent paper for staff development and training, as do Langley (2001) and Pugh et al. (2007). However, one question raised by this study is whether it is sufficient to draw upon research and development work that has mainly been undertaken in large urban hubs in England and abroad, where there are often large LGBT networks, in order to develop good practice in Scotland. Is there a not need for policy makers, service planners and providers to understand what is distinctive about the Scottish context and how local cultures and histories shape the experiences and perspectives of older LGBT people?

Discussion and conclusions

This small Scottish study has highlighted a number of paradoxes and contradictions in terms of identities and categories as well as identifying the need for further work in research, policy and education. I set out to undertake this work (over-)confident that my gender identity would enable me to access and work with these women. This was not the case. While most of the women interviewed saw themselves as women first, they did not see our shared identity as women as sufficient to overcome the risks created by our different sexual identities.

Most of the women interviewed had their friendship networks within the lesbian community. Some spoke about 'comfort zones' being with others of similar identities. But does this categorisation then reinforce 'difference' or is it a necessary strategy meantime? As in any research there are sometimes more questions than answers. What I can say is that as an 'outsider', I have gleaned useful information that has been applied in training situations and materials (Archibald, 2005) and, in a small way, has helped to bridge what is still a divide with further educational work needed. Based upon the findings presented here, of particular relevance to health and social care was the emphasis given to 'families of choice' (including friends and partners both past and present) and the consequent importance of recognising these relationships as family. As with MacKian and Goldring's (Chapter 2) discussion of differences in the gay community, the findings also point to generational differences between lesbians, something that is supported by the existing literature. Tied to this is the need to recognise how a lifetime's worth of experience shapes the way these women negotiate their identities in the present.

Finally, the research highlighted the significance of the interplay of gender with sexuality and age. Compared with (gay) men, these women are likely to live longer, to make greater use of health and social care services and to be less well off in later life (Arber and Ginn, 1994). Their chances of requiring long-stay care are greater than those of gay men but it is also likely that they will approach such services in ways that differ from younger lesbian women and from their heterosexual peers. This illustrates the importance both for research and service provision of considering sexuality in the context of people's lives. I end this chapter with the voice of one of the participants who talks about her own identity.

> CA: You need to be the same as others but also need to be recognised for who you are?

> Yes, recognising difference and that is fine. Don't box me in sister – allow difference but I have to allow your difference too. What I want is to be recognised as a human being, as a female. I want to be treated as any other and recognise that I happen to love a woman that I have loved a woman – that is part of me being me and that is important to me.

CHAPTER 4

Troubles with Bisexuality in Health and Social Care

Rebecca L. Jones

Bisexual people use and work in health and social care services but are often even less visible than lesbian and gay people.[1] In this chapter, I examine some of the reasons for this lack of visibility and argue that it is partly to do with the ways in which bisexuality is a particularly complicated and fluid sexual orientation category. I also illustrate some of the ways in which bisexuality matters and can be relevant in health and social care settings.

The category 'bisexual' appears in the term 'LGBT'. This chapter begins by considering some of the effects of this inclusion in the wider category. I then move on to examine some of the different ways in which bisexuality has been theorised, before introducing some of the ways in which common features of bisexual identities trouble both health and social care practices and notions of the nature of sexual identities. These issues are examined through five case studies involving people who either identify as bisexual or who might be categorised by other people as bisexual.

The disappearing 'B' in LGBT

These days, most organisations, campaigns and publications dealing with non-heterosexual people use the term 'LGBT' ('lesbian, gay, bisexual and trans' or sometimes 'transsexual').[2] The use of this term would seem to indicate an awareness that non-heterosexual people are not just lesbian or gay, but also bisexual and trans. However, the 'B' and 'T' in 'LGBT' often disappear in practice,[3] leaving the focus still on lesbian and gay people (Angelides, 2001).

For example, Stonewall, the campaigning organisation which works for 'equality and justice for lesbians, gay men and bisexuals' (www.stonewall.org. uk) published a major report in 2008 titled *Serves You Right* (Hunt and Dick, 2008). This was the first national survey of LGB experiences of discrimination and 1,658 lesbian, gay and bisexual people in Britain took part. It undoubtedly constitutes an important piece of research. However, bisexual people keep dropping out of the picture. Although the authors state that lesbian, gay and bisexual people were surveyed, the report's subtitle is 'lesbian and gay people's expectations of discrimination' and the word 'bisexual' hardly features in the report. Similarly, another report from Stonewall, about lesbian and bisexual women's experiences of healthcare (Hunt and Fish, 2008) surveyed both lesbians and bisexual women. Of their more than 6,000 respondents, 16% said they were bisexual. The report talks about both lesbians and bisexual women throughout, but the recommendations at the end are things like 'understand lesbian health needs' and 'tell lesbians what they need to know'. Where did the bisexual people go?

Another way in which bisexuality 'disappears' is when famous 'gay' people who have also had significant relationships with people of another sex are cited. For example, Lord Byron and Oscar Wilde are frequently claimed to be gay, despite the fact that both also had significant relationships with women. Liberal Democrat MP Simon Hughes was described as 'secretly gay' and characterised as denying that he was gay by the *Sun* newspaper (Kavanagh, 2006) despite the fact that he consistently said he had had relationships with both men and women. While it is undoubtedly politically important to say that famous people have same-sex relationships, simplifying that to 'they are gay' ends up erasing the other-sex relationships, some of which seem to have been long-lasting, happy, sexual and important.

Why does this keep happening? There are several possible explanations, ranging from the relative political immaturity and hence invisibility of the Bisexual movement, to the history of the sometimes troubled relationships between bisexual people and gay people (Udis-Kessler, 1995), and especially between bisexual women and lesbians in the context of feminism (Armstrong, 1995; Hartman, 2005; Rust, 1992; Rust, 1995). 'The disappearing bisexual' has also been attributed to a wider pattern of fear and misunderstanding of bisexual people (Dobinson *et al.*, 2005; Shokeid, 2001), which is often described as 'biphobia' (Mulick and Wright, 2002; Ochs, 1996; Ochs, 2007). An additional reason for the phenomenon of the disappearing bisexual, I want to suggest, is to do with the ways in which 'bisexual' is particularly complicated and troublesome as an identity category.

Different theorisations of bisexuality

Sexual orientation is commonly theorised in many different, often incompatible, ways and these different theorisations have major implications about how sexuality is researched and what conclusions are drawn (Kauth, 2005). Bisexuality, in particular, has been theorised in a range of ways. There is space here to give only a brief overview of the most important of these, in order to indicate how these theorisations have implications in the world of health and social care practice. (For more nuanced and sophisticated accounts of different theorisations of bisexuality and their implications, see Angelides, 2001; Bowes-Catton, 2007; Carr, 2006; Kauth, 2005; Rodriguez-Rust, 2000.) My intention is not to suggest that any of these theorisations is 'correct' or to be preferred, simply to indicate that they have different implications for what people mean when they talk about bisexuality.

Kinsey's famous studies in the 1940s and 50s (Kinsey *et al.*, 1948, 1953) categorised people's sexual history according to a seven point scale (see Table 4.1).

Table 4.1: The Kinsey Scale

Rating	Description
0	Exclusively heterosexual
1	Predominantly heterosexual, only incidentally homosexual
2	Predominantly heterosexual, but more than incidentally homosexual
3	Equally heterosexual and homosexual
4	Predominantly homosexual, but more than incidentally heterosexual
5	Predominantly homosexual, only incidentally heterosexual
6	Exclusively homosexual
X	Asexual

Kinsey did not focus on questions of sexual identity but on how people behave and on their feelings and desires. As will become apparent, this can be a crucial distinction in relation to bisexuality. His scale has been used by later commentators to complicate the notion that people are either heterosexual, homosexual or bisexual, by using the scale to differentiate between degrees of bisexuality (points 1–5) and to argue that people do not have to be equally attracted to both same-sex and opposite-sex partners (point 3) to count as bisexual.

More recently, Fritz Klein developed Kinsey's work in his Sexual Orientation Grid (Klein, 1993). To fill it in, you put a Kinsey-type number into each box in the grid shown in Table 4.2.

Figure 4.2: The Klein Grid

		Past	Present	Ideal
A	Sexual attraction			
B	Sexual behaviour			
C	Sexual fantasies			
D	Emotional preference			
E	Social preference			
F	Lifestyle			
G	Self-identification			

This grid provides a way of looking at more aspects of sexual identity than Kinsey's original scale. It also distinguishes between past, present and ideal aspects. (For further discussion of the implications of using this sort of grid, see Klein, 1993.) As Klein himself acknowledges, any measurement is unlikely to be exact because sexuality is complex (Petford, 2003). However, for our purposes here, the important thing to note is that the Klein grid complicates the question of what makes up a person's sexual identity and explicitly includes the person's self identification, as well as their behaviours and desires.

Klein also identified four main different types of bisexual people (Klein, 1993):

- transitional bisexuals – who are moving from a heterosexual identity to a lesbian or gay one, or, less commonly, from a lesbian or gay identity to a heterosexual one;
- historical bisexuals – who are now either homosexual or heterosexual but whose pasts include bisexual relationships;
- sequential bisexuals – who have had partners of different sexes at different times in their lifecourse;
- concurrent bisexuals – who are sexually active with both men and women in the same time period.

This typology makes it clear that people's sexual identities may change over the course of their lives. This means that a snapshot at a particular moment in someone's life may not yield the same identity as a lifecourse perspective.

Some theorists argue that 'coming out' is not a linear process that concludes when a person discovers their true and essential identity. They find that sexual identity change is much more common than is generally thought, both among bisexual people (Weinberg *et al.*, 2001) and among the wider population (Diamond, 1998; Rust, 1993). Researchers such as Rodriguez-Rust argue that bisexual identity in particular can be a 'mature state of identity flux' rather than a fixed identity (Rodriguez-Rust, 2007, p. 4).

A final way of theorising bisexual identities is to draw a distinction between bisexual feelings, behaviours and identities, as in Figure 4.1.

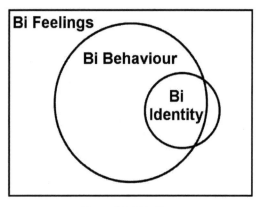

Figure 4.1: Bi-feelings.

It is a consistent research finding that many more people are attracted to people of different genders than behave bisexually, and that more people behave bisexually than identify as bisexual (Rodriguez-Rust, 2000). There is also a small group of people who identify as bisexual, perhaps for reasons of political or personal commitment, but do not behave bisexually. This diagram suggests the importance of distinguishing between which sort of bisexuality is in play in any particular situation, as will become apparent in the later part of this chapter.

Troubles with the category 'bisexual'

Many commentators have noted that the category 'bisexual' is inherently troublesome in a number of ways. The word 'bisexual' implies that there are only two genders, whereas some people who are attracted to people of more than one gender think of gender as a continuum, not an absolute (Barker *et al.*, 2006; Ochs, 2007). Ochs found that as many as a third of her respondents (people who are attracted to both men and women but don't describe themselves as bisexual) said that they rejected the label 'bisexual' because it implied that there are only two genders (Ochs, 2007). The word 'bisexual' also implies that the division between men and women is the most important factor in sexual choice. Some people say that the gender of their sexual partners is irrelevant and that calling themselves 'bisexual' is therefore misleading (Barker *et al.*, 2008).

Some of Ochs' respondents also rejected the label 'bisexual' because they felt it emphasised sex, not relationships, by having the word 'sexual' within it. They pointed out that the categories 'gay' or 'lesbian' do not emphasise sex in this manner (Ochs, 2007, p. 80). Other people argue that the term 'bisexual' leads to a binary understanding of sexuality where bisexuality is partly homosexuality and partly heterosexuality (Rodriguez-Rust, 2000, p. xvi), and would prefer to theorise it as a discrete sexual identity. However, while acknowledging these difficulties and complexities, I continue to use the category 'bisexual' as a useful umbrella term for people who experience attraction to people of both the same and other genders than themselves (Firestein, 2007, p. xx).[4]

Case studies

In the case studies that follow, I focus on three ways in which common features of bisexuality can complicate notions of the nature of sexual identities, and how this can have implications for health and social care. These are that, firstly, bisexuality is a particularly 'invisible' sexual identity – it is often overlooked as a possible sexual orientation and people are assumed to be really homosexual or heterosexual. Secondly, people who have attractions to or relationships with people of the same and different genders than themselves, either at the same time or over the course of their lives, may not describe themselves as bisexual. Thirdly, non-mainstream relationship patterns are more common among bisexual people and this can have implications when they use health and social care services.

First, a word about the provenance of these case studies. They are not based on particular individuals who took part in research studies. Rather, they are composites, based on the findings of a variety of research studies and also on real life situations known to members of the UK bisexual community. All the case studies have been reviewed by at least 25 people who are active in the UK bisexual community and by UK academics doing research into bisexuality. This review process took place partly online and partly during a workshop at BiReCon 2008 – a conference for academics and practitioners held as part of the annual national bisexual gathering, BiCon 2008 (www. bicon.org.uk/). These reviewers helped refine the case studies and agreed that they are plausible, authentic, realistic and, in some instances, common.

CASE STUDY – MEL

Mel works in a care home for adults with severe physical and learning difficulties. She likes her job even though it is often extremely challenging and very tiring. She gets on well with most of her colleagues and they help each other to cope with the difficult bits of the work. She has been living with her partner, Cleo, since before she started this job. Her colleagues seem to deal okay with her having a female partner and Cleo even went along to a few work socials with some of the other partners. After a difficult few months, Cleo and Mel split up and Cleo moved out. Mel was quite upset but some of her colleagues were supportive and helped her to come to terms with the break up. Mel's colleagues had assumed that she is a lesbian but she actually identifies as bisexual. She has never mentioned this because it didn't seem immediately relevant when she was seeing Cleo, and she was worried about how they would react. After a few months she started seeing someone else, Martin. Eventually her colleagues find out about her new partner. She picks up that there is a lot of gossip about her going around and a few people make jokey comments to her about her 'coming back to join us' and that all she needed was the love of a good man. One colleague says that she always thought Mel was really straight and it must have just been a phase she was going through. Mel starts to feel really uncomfortable at work and no longer feels supported by her colleagues when service users behave challengingly. In the end this leads to her leaving the job because she can't cope with its stresses when she is not feeling supported by her colleagues.

This case study exemplifies how people's lack of awareness of the possibility that someone might be bisexual can create difficulties for individuals. Bisexuality could be described as an invisible identity, in this sense. Mel's colleagues have assumed that she is a lesbian because she had a female partner and, when this relationship ends and her new partner is a man, they assume that she is now, or indeed always really was, heterosexual. Such assumptions are perhaps not surprising, given the prevalence of the idea that people are either heterosexual or homosexual and the consequent tendency to equate someone's sexual identity with their current relationship, if they are monogamous. As Ochs argues:

A quiet bisexual will be assumed to be either heterosexual or homosexual. To avoid being mislabelled, a bisexual woman must declare her bisexuality and risk being seen as aggressively and inappropriately flaunting her orientation. (Ochs, 2007, p. 76)

It is perhaps because she does not want to be seen to be making an unnecessary fuss about her sexual identity that Mel has let her colleagues assume that she is a lesbian.

The comments her colleagues make about Mel 'coming back to join *us*', just needing to meet the right man, and positioning same-sex relationships as a phase, also highlight the latent homophobia of even workplaces that are apparently accepting of non-heterosexual relationships. The nature of Mel's work means that supportive and friendly relationships with colleagues are particularly important. These comments contribute to Mel's feeling that she is not accepted by her colleagues and her subsequent inability to cope with the challenges of her demanding job.

CASE STUDY – GREG

Greg has been seriously depressed on and off for years. He has tried various medical treatments with limited success. One time when he visited his GP, she suggested he try talking therapies and referred him on to a counsellor. Initially, Greg found the sessions quite useful. He felt he was discovering new things about himself and learning new ways of thinking about old problems. One time he mentioned that, although he has only ever had relationships with women, he has always been attracted to men too and sometimes looks at gay porn on the Internet. His counsellor seemed to consider this really significant but from this point on, Greg found their sessions much less useful. He felt as if the counsellor had decided that he is really gay and was trying to get him to admit it to himself. Greg is quite comfortable with the fact that he is attracted to men but doesn't want to do anything more about it at the moment. He really likes women too and hopes to form another relationship with a woman in the future. He has never really labelled his own sexuality. Greg started to wonder whether his counsellor was right and he is 'really' gay and just not admitting it to himself. This made his depression get worse and he stopped going to see the counsellor, telling his GP that counselling just wasn't right for him.

However, a couple of years later, Greg made a new friend, Angus, who described himself as bisexual. Angus had also seen a counsellor for some years and said that this particular person was really good and had helped him to understand what it meant to him to be bi. Greg decided to give counselling another try and made an appointment to see her. This time it worked much better for him. He concluded that perhaps he was bisexual but that his bisexuality still wasn't an issue to him, and they didn't talk about it very much once he had decided that. However, this left him feeling free to talk about the issues that did underlie his depression. After some months, Greg found he was feeling considerably less depressed.

In this case, lack of awareness of bisexuality as a possible sexual orientation meant that something which was neither problematic nor particularly important to Greg was given an unhelpful significance by his first counsellor. His counsellor didn't seem to consider the possibility of bisexuality and certainly didn't mention it to Greg. Research suggests that this is all too common (Page, 2007; Petford, 2003; Smiley, 1997). This lack of awareness of bisexuality as a possible sexual orientation is particularly significant given that there is some evidence of worse mental health for bisexual adults than homosexual adults (Dodge and Sandfort, 2007; Jorm *et al.*, 2002) and than the general population (Balsam *et al.*, 2005).

Once he had found a counsellor who seemed to be more aware of bisexuality, and to accept Greg's own assessment that this wasn't the issue that underlay his depression, he was able to benefit from talking therapies. It should be noted that Greg's access to a counsellor with a better understanding of bisexuality did not come from health and social care services, like his first referral via his GP, but from informal contact with someone who had an identity as bisexual.

CASE STUDY – MURIEL

Muriel is 78. When she was a girl she had a series of intense 'crushes' on older girls but she met her husband-to-be when she was 18 and quickly fell in love with him. They got married and had three children. When Muriel was in her early 30s, her husband divorced her.

When she was in her late 30s Muriel joined a women's consciousness-raising group. In the group she came across the idea of lesbianism, which she had never heard discussed before, and she met a woman, Pat, who already identified as a lesbian. Muriel was strongly attracted to her and before long they had started a relationship. After Muriel's children had left home, they lived together for several years, and became a familiar couple on the local lesbian scene. Pat developed breast cancer and, after many difficult months, she died. Muriel got a lot of support from her circle of lesbian friends and from a local voluntary organisation which supported lesbians and gay men who had been bereaved.

Some months later, to her astonishment, she fell in love with a man, Colin. Her friends were very disapproving of her new relationship and gradually cut contact with her. The new relationship flourished, although Muriel recognised that she was still attracted to women too and missed her old circle of friends, especially as she was still grieving for Pat. She didn't feel able to keep using the bereavement service because she no longer seemed to count as a lesbian.

In the mid-1980s, Muriel came across the idea of 'bisexuality' and started calling herself bisexual. After some years, the relationship with Colin ended amicably and Muriel met another woman, Joan, and went back to thinking of herself as lesbian because that was Joan's identity and she expected this to be the final relationship of her life.

Last year Joan died and Muriel experienced some major health problems. She started receiving home care. She gets on well with one of her regular carers who asked her about the photos she had up around the house of her former partners. Muriel answers honestly but is horrified to discover later that her carer has spread malicious gossip among her colleagues about her past, saying that Muriel had been sexually predatory and promiscuous.

Over the course of a relatively long life, Muriel had relationships with both men and women. She identified variously as heterosexual, lesbian and bisexual. Such movements between identity labels are relatively common among women who have been sexually attracted to people of more than one gender (George, 1993; Ochs, 2007; Rust, 1995). Which identity she drew on at a particular time depended not only on the person she was in a relationship with, but also on the social circles she was moving in, the wider political climate and the ideas about sexuality to which she had access. Like Mel, Muriel found that the support available to her to help her cope with traumatic life events depended on her displaying an 'acceptable' sexual identity. When Pat died she needed a bereavement support service that understood the additional issues of having lost a same-sex partner, but she did not feel able to continue to use the lesbian and gay bereavement service because she was now in a relationship with a man. Since she did not have a social group who identified as bisexual or who were sympathetic to her bisexual identity, she only experienced support when she identified as lesbian or heterosexual.

Once Muriel started receiving health and social care services in her own home, her past relationships with both men and women became the source of unpleasant gossip among her carers, a problem also experienced by some of the participants in the study carried out by Dobinson, MacDonnell *et al.* in 2005. People who behave bisexually are often seen as greedy, promiscuous and predatory, a phenomenon which is claimed to be part of a wider biphobia (George, 1993; Mulick and Wright, 2002; Ochs, 1996; Ochs, 2007).

> **CASE STUDY – ANNE**
>
> Anne's first child, Luca, has been born six weeks early. Luca is in Special Care because of breathing difficulties and low birth weight. Anne has three partners, all of whom think of themselves as having a parental role – she is married to Jonti, Mark is the baby's biological father and Lara is also going to be extensively involved in bringing up the child. Lara was present at the birth but Mark and Jonti were not because the labour was very quick and they could not get to the hospital in time. The Special Care Baby Unit has a policy that only parents can visit their children while they are in the Unit. The hospital has assumed that Jonti is Luca's father because he is Anne's husband. Anne is terrified about whether Luca is going to be alright and wants all her partners to see him so they will feel involved in his care and she will feel supported by their involvement. Lara was very moved by the experience of supporting Anne in labour and seeing Luca being born. She is now feeling bereft at him being taken away to somewhere she cannot see him. Mark is feeling angry about not being allowed to see his son, and is thinking of storming up to a nurse and shouting 'I am the father', but doesn't want to upset Anne by creating a scene. Jonti is longing to see Luca too, but feels a bit guilty that he should be the one allowed to visit when he is neither the biological father nor the person who was present at the birth.

Anne is in what is often described as a 'polyamorous' or 'poly' relationship – negotiated, consensual non-monogamy. Many bisexual people are monogamous, but poly relationships are more often found among people who identify as bisexual than among other groups (for further discussion, see Anderlini-D'Onofrio, 2004; Weitzman, 2007 and the special issue of the journal *Sexualities*: Haritaworn *et al.*, 2006), so it can be an important issue for bisexual people using health and social care services. In this case, the hospital's definitions of who counts as a parent does not map onto the family's ideas and this creates unnecessary distress at what is already a stressful time.

Using case studies to explore bisexuality

In this chapter I have illustrated some of the ways in which bisexuality matters in health and social care settings. The case studies I have presented have emphasised some of the difficulties that may be experienced by bisexual service users and care workers due to others' lack of knowledge or unhelpful conceptualisations of what is meant by bisexuality. Change is needed at many different levels, from the strategic and organisational to the personal and emotional, if health and social care services are to be made accessible and acceptable to all people who have some relationship to the identity 'bisexual'. One important way in which care can be improved is by providing training and education to front-line care workers and their managers. Within a training and education programme, case studies such as these can provide a useful resource.

Summaries of people's experiences, based on real life, and presented in the form of a story can be a particularly effective way of presenting unfamiliar issues (Northedge, 2002). They can introduce a complex topic in a way that it unthreatening because it appears to be 'just about people'. They can provide concrete examples of apparently abstract issues which are grounded in everyday practice. They can provide a way of moving beyond fixed categories and thinking critically about them.

Case studies such as these can form the basis of discussion by asking participants to relate the stories to their personal experience and practice. Participants could address such questions as:

1. Do you think the person in this case study would describe themselves as bisexual?
   - In what circumstances might it be helpful to use the word 'bisexual' to describe their identity?
   - In what circumstances might it be unhelpful to use the word 'bisexual' to describe their identity?

2. How could things have worked out better for the person in the case study?
   - What could the care worker involved have done to help?
   - What could the care organisation do to make a better outcome more likely?

3. Have you ever met someone like the person in this case study?
   - In what ways was their situation similar or different to the case study?
   - What happened for them?
   - What did you do?
   - Is there anything you wish you could have done?
   - Are there any ways you could help there to be a better outcome next time you meet someone in this situation?

Conclusions

There are, of course, many situations in which bisexuality is non-problematic or beneficial in health and social care. In particular, care workers who identify as bisexual, such as Mel, may constitute a valuable resource within organisations, since they may have the skills and experience both to raise awareness generally of bisexual issues and to work sensitively with bisexual service users. They may also be well placed to work with both heterosexual and homosexual service users, since they may have a good understanding of a range of different social networks.

There are, nonetheless, situations in which bisexual practitioners experience problems in health and care settings due to a lack of understanding of bisexuality. Given the relative invisibility of bisexual identities, colleagues are likely to have wrongly assumed that an individual is either heterosexual or lesbian/ gay, on the basis of a current partner. Such an assumption may be especially problematic given the emotional demands made on many front-line care workers in the course of their day-to-day work, which makes the support of colleagues particularly important.

Bisexuality is also relevant when service users either identify as bisexual (like Anne and her partners, and Muriel at some points of her life) or have some relationship to bisexuality without so identifying (like Greg, and Muriel at other points in her life). Service providers' lack of understanding of bisexuality can create real difficulties in making services accessible and appropriate for bisexual people.

While some of these difficulties can be at least partially addressed by training and general awareness-raising activities (for specific suggestions in relation to health, see Dobinson *et al.*, 2005), I have also argued in this chapter that the relative complexity of bisexuality as an identity category makes this a more challenging task. How bisexuality is theorised affects how the categories work – at the most straightforward level, practitioners need to ask: are we talking about behaviour, identity or feelings here? The difference between these different theorisations of bisexuality can have major implications for service users and care providers. Someone who behaves bisexually but does not use that label to describe themselves is unlikely to use a service aimed at LGBT people, for example.

However, the relative complexity of the category 'bisexual' also carries benefits for care providers aiming to improve the accessibility and effectiveness of services. Since many bisexual people have changed the sexual identity label they use, and since bisexuality carries such various meanings, remembering the 'B' in LGBT can help care providers to remain aware of the provisional and fluid nature of all sexual identity categories.

Notes

1. The issue for trans people is less often one of invisibility: see Firestein, B. (Ed.) (2007) for a discussion of bisexual invisibility.
2. See the chapter by Alleyn and Jones in this book for discussion of some of the differences between 'transexual' and 'transgender', which create the need for the more inclusive abbreviation 'trans'. Other terms, such as 'LGBTQI' – lesbian, gay, bisexual, trans, queer and intersex – are also used but much less commonly in the UK.
3. In this chapter I focus specifically on the disappearance of bisexuality within the category LGBT because some of the issues are distinctive to bisexual people. Similar, but also distinctive, issues are involved in the disappearance of trans from the category, but they are beyond the scope of this chapter. It should also be noted that there is significant overlap between the two categories – about 20% of people attending BiCon, the main national gathering for UK bisexuals, do not identify straightforwardly as male or female (Barker *et al.*, 2008).
4. This definition is intended to be inclusive of trans people by not implying that there are only two genders.

CHAPTER 5

Queerying Care: Dissident Trans Identities in Health and Social Care Settings

Chrissy Alleyn and Rebecca L. Jones

So God created man in his own image... male and female created he them. (Genesis Chapter1, verse 27)

If only we could all re-learn to speak out of our common suffering and need we would be surprised to find how close we are to one another. (Laurens van der Post)

Are you sitting comfortably? Then I'll begin...

Once upon a time, far far away, there lived a beautiful princess. Sadly she was trapped in the body of a fourteen stone bin-man from Crewe.

That is the fairy story that medical gender specialists and transsexual people developed to justify a pragmatic course of often life-saving treatment: 'gender reassignment'. It is a fairy story in the sense that it is a plausible simplification of a more complex truth, thought necessary because it is feared that the truth is unpalatable.

Who is speaking here?

This chapter draws on both academic literature and personal experience. Although both Rebecca Jones and Chrissy Alleyn contributed to this chapter, the 'I' that speaks in this chapter is Chrissy Alleyn, who combines academic knowledge with personal experience of the subject matter.

What, then, are my credentials to talk about dissident trans identities in health and social care? My academic credentials include Masters level study of modern transgender, as part of which I reviewed in the region of a thousand relevant websites, blogs and message boards. My activist credentials are that I worked for two years as a union Equalities Officer for a County Council and am currently engaged in high-profile trans activism within Traveller communities. This means I have interviewed perhaps 100 trans people on varied aspects of their lives. My personal credentials are that I am a radical trans person, gender disidentified (don't identify as any gender), who has had genital surgery. After I transitioned to the social role of female I waited seven years for surgery, the first five of them without hormones, and finally received counselling nine months *after* my surgery. My experience is not unique. Although I have provided references wherever possible within this chapter, there are places where I have relied on my own extensive experience and research.

Introduction

Although most people have heard of transsexuality, relatively few know much about it. Individuals may use labels differently, but a transsexual person is generally one who has moved or is moving from one clearly defined sex/gender category to another through the vehicle of surgery, male to female or female to male, and is likely to identify as female or male (respectively). Genital surgery is one of many procedures they may undergo to cement this shift, and they may seek breast enlargement or reduction, brow or jaw reduction, vocal chord shortening, hair transplant or removal and, in some cases, forearm shortening.

Until the last decade or so transsexuals were likely to conceal their history, but now many trans people are becoming more open about their histories and more likely to identify themselves in complex ways. It is common now for a range of people who may or may not be seeking surgery to use the prefix 'trans'. A Transman is usually a person who was ascribed female at birth, a Transwoman one who was ascribed male, but the crucial difference from the fairy story version is that they may not be seeking full (or any) gender reassignment surgery. Trans people, in this sense, are people whose gender identity has changed, but it may not have changed to a simple 'male' or 'female'.

A growing number of trans people are becoming increasingly dissatisfied with the fairy story, and the attendant diagnosis and prognosis, and are finding new ways of understanding and inhabiting their bodies. Some trans people are working out their own formulations of their identities, their own sets of gender-free pronouns, and their own understanding of their aetiology (causative factors) and diagnostic features. They may describe themselves as trans or transgender, or they may use other identity labels, such as 'genderqueer' or just 'queer'. These trans people have dissident trans identities, by which I mean that they do not identify unproblematically as one or another sex or gender.

In this sense, trans or transgender are terms that can be applied to people who haven't made a binary (either or) shift, or who may move around within, between or outside the traditional sex/gender categories. This mobility is based on evidence that masculine or feminine sex and gender aren't exclusive categories but ends of a continuum. Within this community of differently gendered people, sometimes referred to in the broadest sense by the term 'gender community', the 'traditional' transsexual can come to be viewed as relatively conservative.

This chapter describes a minority movement emerging from within trans activism and writing. This movement is very influential and is having a profound and polarising impact on the gender community. It challenges the absolute validity of the traditional view of transsexuality and offers alternatives with wide-ranging implications.

The distinction between 'sex' and 'gender' (see Glossary) is important to understanding transsexuality and dissident trans identities. 'Sex' refers to a person's physical body, whereas 'gender' refers to their social behaviour. A transsexual person gains a surgical referral by claiming to be in the wrong *social* body (to 'really' be a woman trapped in a man's body, for example), but there is a growing body of evidence indicating that, for a sizeable proportion, the problem is less social than *physical*. Many trans people do not feel trapped in the wrong body; they feel they are in their own bodies which are the wrong shape (Lawrence, 2006). The treatment protocols demand that one 'successfully' live in role (the 'Real Life Test') for one or two years before being approved for surgery, but for many it is the breasts or genitals that are the problem, not that they prefer coffee mornings to fixing the car (or vice versa). In a striking parallel to Alien Limb Syndrome, perception of one's body, the mental image of self we all have, does not map onto the actual body, and the only sufficient and proven therapy is to modify the body (Prosser, 1998). Unfortunately the current diagnostic and referral process conceals this anomaly within the fairytale trope (Barrett, 2007).

In order to obtain medical treatment and recognition, trans people have to conform to current diagnostic protocols for transsexuality. These include clearly imagining onself to be the 'opposite' gender and consistently and permanently behaving and living as the 'opposite' gender. The dissident trans movement is very critical of these protocols, claiming that people are being thrust from one ill-fitting and arbitrary category to another in order to satisfy social convention.

However not all trans people accept this critique. Instead, they argue that, on the whole, the current protocols work and improve people's lives, any change will inevitably be for the worse, and people who have what they want from medical services could at least have the decency not to rock the boat.

Transsexuals are rare, in the region of one in ten thousand of the population. But imagine how many people you will see in the course of your life – at least one will be trans (seeing ten new people a day for three years should just about do it). If you work with a trans person as client or colleague, or know one as friend or family, you will already be aware that a little understanding of the issues surrounding trans lives makes interactions with trans people much easier. One's sex is a key classificatory category for state and social interactions and permeates every aspect of our lives, from passports to pensions to prisons, toilets to tennis-matches to dinner-party table settings. To somebody with a dissident view of their sex this is a constant, relentless irritation; people with a moderate knowledge of key concepts will find interactions with trans people far less stressful.

To this end, the rest of this chapter is a lightning tour of some of the key ideas within transgender, focusing particularly on the implications of dissident trans identities in health and social care settings. Having already introduced 'the transsexual fairy-story' and a number of key identity words, I start by describing the history of sex categories and their logic. I introduce an alternative logic that has come out of trans-activism and feminist study: that the bodies described as male and female are not two separate categories, but two ends of one continuum. Having introduced these key concepts, I briefly overview the state of the academic literature on trans issues. I then introduce key ideas that describe how identity is made and used and the impact this can have on relationships. The final sections of the chapter detail a representative (but not exhaustive) selection of issues faced by gender dissident people within health and social care settings, and suggest strategies for improving services.

Sexing the body

According to many traditions there were created two, and *only* two, sexes, and you were one or the other depending on what role you performed in the production of children. Although this was a reasonable view, it was by no means a universal one; other nations, tribes and cultures traditionally categorised people into at least three sexes/genders. These categorisations sometimes included intersex and transgender people as a supernumerary gender, sometimes as one of the three primary genders which appeared commonly enough to be assigned important ceremonial and social roles (Bullough and Bullough, 1993; Eliade, 2004; Herdt, 1998). Over time, however, the first story became very popular, to the degree that everyone in the world, pretty much, now believes the Story of the Two Sexes (Conner *et al.*, 1997; Feinberg, 1996).

This story, that there are two, and only two, sexes, is a story we are told so often, and have been told for so long, that we all firmly believe it, *without critically examining the evidence*. Of course it doesn't help that the evidence has been 'Sexed Up' to reinforce the failing categories. Anyone who fails to meet the criteria – has an 'oversized' clitoris or 'undersized' penis, mixed sexual characteristics, a chromosomal or hormonal 'anomaly' – has, until recently, been surgically or hormonally rationalised upon diagnosis, often at birth (commonly by removal of the clitoris). The parents were left in no doubt by unimpeachable experts – doctors – about the serious social implications of this biological 'failure' and in the main felt they had no choice but to comply (Fausto-Sterling, 2000). This disquieting praxis is of modifying bodies to fit an elegant theory, rather than the more rigorous process of making a theory that fits the facts.

Determining someone's sex is not always as straightforward as we might assume. Traditional binary understandings of sex are unable to answer the questions posed by real bodies:

1. Is an impotent man a *real* man?
2. Is a man with a tiny penis (a 'micro-phallus') a real man?
3. Does it matter or not whether it works, whether he has children?
4. Is a (potent) man who sleeps with men a real man?
5. Is a man who lost his penis in an accident a real man?
6. Is a man born with two working penises *more* of a man?
7. Is a man born with no penis a real man?
8. Is a man born with a clitoris a real man?
9. Is a man who was born a woman a real man?

ACTIVITY

Look back at this list and see where you stopped saying 'Of course *he* is'. That may tell you something about how you personally define sex/ gender.

> Ask yourself why you chose that particular point, how on a sliding scale of real living bodies you could decide a quantitative, either/or, shift had been made.
>
> How did you make that attribution, when you have no access to the relevant organs for verification?
>
> Given your answers to the questions above, how do you think this will affect the way you respond to trans people?

Male and female genitals can be so similar that they are mistaken; the difference between the sexes isn't clear-cut (Fausto-Sterling, 2000). By any measure, hormonal, chromosomal, anatomical, social, behavioural, there is no absolute dividing line where one sex stops and the next starts (Nataf, 1995). In fact there is marked overlap, to the degree that the International Olympic Committee's sex testing programme has been under considerable criticism since the 1980s.

At the Beijing Olympics '1 in 500 gender tests were expected to reveal abnormalities' (Macartney and Garlick, 2008). Biologist Alison Carlson states '...male and female are really a biological continuum. We're so much more alike than different. It is culture that makes us see sex as black and white.' Ursula Mittwoch, Emeritus Professor of developmental biology, calls sex tests 'unscientific' and says she can think of no scientist who supports them. 'The binary male/female classification places insufficient emphasis on biological variation' (quoted in Vines, 1992). Whatever gender or sex determining test is used, some people will fail the test, some results will be inconclusive, and some people will get different results every time they test. Some women will test as men, some will test as neither, and some will test as both.

Academic literature

This more nuanced understanding of the nature of sex and gender is not found throughout the academic literature on trans issues. Surgical or psychiatric texts usually focus on transsexuality and describe it in pathological terms as a series of conditions (Barrett, 2007; Tully, 1992). Psychological literature tends to plead for acceptance through the rhetoric of normalcy overlying extreme distress (Bloom, 2002; Moon, 2008). Social work texts look at damage limitation in difficult circumstances – the difficult circumstances usually being transgender (Israel and Tarver, 1997; Mallon, 1999).

In more sociological academic literature there is often a more radical understanding of sex/gender variability. Fausto-Sterling's (2000) *Sexing the Body* critically examines the medical and social construction of the sex categories, highlighting the practice of surgery to align troublesome intersex bodies to social standards. Radical trans and queer literature treat the fluidity of sex/gender/sexual orientation and the inadequacy of categories as a given (Bornstein, 1995; Feinberg, 1996; Hines, 2007).

In the second wave of trans biographies, particularly following the influence of Kate Bornstein, Leslie Feinberg and Sandy Stone, trans people looking to find themselves in print have discovered a problematisation of binary genders and an expanding cloud of fluid identities (Stone, 1991; Bornstein, 1995; Rothblatt, 1995; Feinberg, 1996; Webb, 1996; Griggs, 1998; O'Keefe and Fox, 2003). Trans people generally construct their identities from the materials at hand and the materials are getting a lot queerer. This is particularly noticeable in the fluid categories sometimes found among queer youth.

Now I have critically examined the evidence for the two-sex model I hope I have shown some of the ways it is inadequate. So we can abandon the model under certain circumstances. How far might we stretch those circumstances?

Identity labels

There are a number of people who cannot, or choose not to, fit the two-sex model. They might identify as trans, transgender, transsexual, queer, genderqueer, bi-gender, intersex or by another such term. These terms are how people identify themselves, or are identified by others. Identity words are a contextual and partial response to a specific question – who/what are you? In this context I self identify with the term TransDyke Queer; my *sex* is trans, my *sexual orientation* dyke, my *gender* queer. In the context of a builders' yard I would probably identify as male, at a party I would most likely be found with the women.

When we use identity terms we use ones we believe will be understood or believed, which are appropriate within the context of the question, which we use to give *as specific* and *as truthful* an interpretation of ourselves as we can, or wish to. We may use these terms for short- or long-term aims, we may use them inconsistently or fraudulently, discarding or modifying them as necessary, and they need not represent a definitive statement of our self-identity (Warnke, 2007).

If traditional identities do not describe us we are free to invent new ones (or revive old ones). The problem with identifying oneself by a new term is that few people understand it. By the time you've described what it means, time has passed, and the session you scheduled to sort out a problem has gone. Next time you might see a different practitioner and have to start all over again. Being trans is clearly a powerful motive for simplifying – telling fairytales.

Health and social care settings

When a person with a dissident sexual or gender identity engages with health or caring services we will frame the identity we project around what we hope to gain in treatment, our reading of bias and level of understanding in that service, our reading of the beliefs of the practitioner, whether we are there voluntarily, and how voluntarily.

When the practitioner engages with a gender dissident the tendency is to classify the person by binary sex/gender. This might be because of past experience, for diagnostic or treatment purposes, or more likely as a result of being embedded in a world where there are exactly two sexes. It may be that as a result both perpetuate the fairy story. It may be that the dissident declines to engage further, or the practitioner terminates the contact, perhaps finding the client challenging or unsuited to their services.

For trans people obtaining a medical solution is dependent on behaviour, dress, employment status, physical fitness, attendance at appointments, and telling the right story, and it is never clear who is a gate-keeper and who a care-provider; who might give help; who could block treatment; who can safely be told the truth.

In the sections that follow I discuss issues commonly arising for trans people within health and social care settings. My particular focus is on the issues faced by people with dissident trans identities, but in order to elaborate these, I also cover some of the issues faced by trans people in general, including those with more traditional transsexual identities.

One general point is worth mentioning here: trans people are likely to experience severe challenges when they have changed their birth records. Their credit history will be erased, all government enquiries about tax or benefits need to be redirected to specially trained personnel, resulting in delays and unwanted attention, cases being lost in the system, and general unaccount-ability. Trans people may have problems with phone services, financial – using debit or credit cards – or services where confidentiality is an issue, when vocal range or appearance does not match personal details. Some dissident trans people have changed their birth records to make clear a break from their birth-assigned gender. However that may not mean they align unproblemati-cally, or at all, with the new gender. All these problems can be directly relevant or have knock-on effects in health and social care settings.

Specialist medical practitioners

Specialist medical practitioners – those working in gender clinics, or perform-
ing specialist surgery – tend to be more understanding of dissident trans
identities in person than in print and to judge outcomes on patient satisfac-
tion rather than convention. They are often under considerable pressure
(from medical academia, the General Medical Council, and their managers)
to represent outcomes in a normative medical framework (the fairy story).
But if a client is well adjusted, happy, and willing to conform minimally to
the conditions for referral, gender specialists may be willing to support their
reassignment regardless of their evident dissidence.

Non-specialist health practitioners

However, before a trans person can see a specialist, they have to be referred
on by non-specialist health practitioners, typically GPs. It has been widely
reported that non-specialist health professionals tend to have stereotypical views of transsexuality and gender dysphoria, and '[some] professionals
remain opposed to hormonal or surgical reassignment' (Green, 1999). I also
have found that although some GPs have attended specialist seminars, these
were generally framed within the fairy story. The general lack of awareness
of protocols combined with stereotypical views leads to confusion over
hormone regimens or a flat refusal to prescribe. It can also lead to confusion
over which procedures are cosmetic and which will be funded, and uneven
referrals sometimes to unqualified or inexperienced specialists and surgeons.
I have found many GPs to be open and understanding of dissidence in person,
yet unwilling to support or refer requests for funded treatments to managers
or other departments.

Whether a trans person is able to access specialist services depends on the
funding criteria in their particular area of the country. Funders' criteria vary;
one area's non-essential cosmetic procedure is another's standard practice. Dr
J. Barrett is the current director of the UK's only state-funded gender clinic
at Charing Cross in London. It is Barrett's view that a trans person would not
get funding for first referral to a gender clinic if they did not act like one or
the other gender consistently enough (Barrett, 2008).

The limited numbers of specifically trained psychiatrists available to local
mental health teams can lead to delays in the first referral from non-specialist
services to a gender clinic. Non-specialist psychiatrists tend to have stereotypical views and are time consuming to brief, especially if they are on rotation.
Non-stereotypical gender presentation might be diagnosed as a symptom of

psychosis, and genital dysphoria as generalised dissatisfaction or non-specific mental illness amenable to psychiatric intervention (Barrett, 2007).

There appears to be no general awareness of guidelines on who should commission or provide which services, such as pre- or post-surgical counselling, and when and in what order they should be provided. I know of several cases (75% of my surgical cohort, including myself) where the local psychiatric services assumed the gender clinic was providing counselling while they in turn expected local services to have put something in place. One would think that pre-surgical counselling might be rather important for an elective procedure to remove one's penis.

At a more mundane level, neglecting the importance of something as simple as a pronoun can result in unwanted attention when prescriptions are collected or patients called. Practices may be slow or unwilling to change Mr to Ms or vice versa on their records, databases do not accommodate a third option, and that information is sometimes used to select for regular screening for gender-specific conditions, so 'cannot be changed'. What exactly does that term *gender-specific conditions* mean when faced with somebody who needs both breast and prostate examinations?

Social and caring services

Access to and custody of children is a commonly mentioned issue for many trans people. Strong evidence suggests that continuity of contact from the earliest age is likely to lead to the best outcomes for parents and children in trans families. Professor Richard Green, the previous director of Charing Cross Gender Identity Clinic and world-renowned expert, was a frequent witness propounding this view.

> I am saddened at the number of cases in which I have testified as an expert witness where children and transsexual parent have been denied the opportunity to continue their parent–child relationship. From the many cases I have seen, a transsexual parent does not have a deleterious effect on the children. (Green, 1999)

Trans people have problems getting access to looked-after children; ignorance or discrimination within social work settings can cause tensions with the foster or adoptive parents and children. This is even more the case for people with dissident trans identities. Courts are more likely to be biased against the trans parent when being transgendered is seen by a case-worker to be problematic. This was certainly the case in my seven-year struggle to see my daughter, and my experience is borne out by the three senior social work practitioner/trainers and a score of practitioners I corresponded with during my time as County Council Union Equalities Officer (2005–7).

Of concern are the widespread reports of transphobia by staff within the social and caring services; these may implicate colleagues or indicate deeper institutionalised transphobic values. But there is continual improvement, and recent changes in the law (i.e. Sex Discrimination (Gender Reassignment) Regulations 1999, Gender Recognition Act 2004, Gender Equality Duty 2007) have made local government and public sector bodies such as the health service more responsible for ensuring systematic equalities training.

Solutions?

Most practitioners are working within the fairytale 'A trapped in B's body', while gender dissidents and some specialists are developing a sex/gender variance 'either/neither/both' model (Barrett, 2007). Trans people presenting at health or care settings may view themselves as 'either/neither/both', but will generally represent themselves as 'A trapped in B's body', just in case. They will then be under pressure to maintain this position through the referral process to maintain credibility. This distortion of data has contributed to the transsexual diagnosis and treatment remaining relatively unchanged for 80 years. Can you imagine if the same were true for lung cancer, heart disease, HIV? There are ways to overcome this inertia – *by including trans people in significant processes.*

Employing transgendered professionals in specialist units has been productive, enabling the unit to benefit from informal advice and criticism, and the service users to feel they will be understood (Green, 1999; Namaste, 2000). But there is a general trend among trans people to dislike working in non-specialist care settings, often citing institutional homophobia or transphobia. There is also a tendency to recruit 'traditional' transsexuals, which sends a very clear message to dissidents.

Support groups and organisations, commonly administered and funded by trans people and friends, could be mainstreamed by funded care providers. The providers would benefit from the training opportunities and data. Many would particularly benefit from some pronoun awareness. However the three largest UK advocacy and support groups (the Beaumont Society, the Gender Trust and Press For Change) are conservative in nature and their literature and advice cannot be applied uncritically (or in certain cases, at all) to dissident trans people.

Practitioners should consider the role of advocacy in their work with trans people. Trans people may be at considerable risk, especially if they are housed in a problematic area. Most people do not understand the urgency of a trans person facing hate crime, which will probably end in violence and possibly death. This is particularly a concern for non-passing trans people and dissidents and may not apply to transsexuals who can pass as traditionally gendered (Namaste, 2000).

It is my view that a significant number of 'traditional' transsexuals are so because they do not know there are alternatives. Many pre-operative transsexuals aggressively defend the trope of 'girl trapped in boy's body' primarily because it is the only safe thing to say. Asking them open questions, such as 'So how do you describe your gender?', is more likely to elicit valuable responses than closed questions like 'So what makes you believe you are a woman?'.

Working with trans people as researcher and transactivist I find it helpful to spot and respond to cues. When a person uses terms like Trans, Queer, Genderqueer, Transgender, TransDyke, Boi or Grrrl for instance, they are saying that they don't believe in the two-sex model, and they don't feel you should either, at least when dealing with them.

When a trans person asks you where the toilet is you may find it worthwhile to have thought through some options beforehand. What would you suggest for a male-bodied feminine gendered person? Male body – male loo? Are there unisex facilities, would a disabled loo be offensive, would other women be offended if they used the Ladies?

As a general rule of thumb do *not* initially suggest the sex that the person has *come from*, even if you cannot really say for certain which gender or sex they are *going to*. Urinary segregation, with the division of toilets into male or female and the violent or confrontational penalties for non-conformity, raises issues for the majority of trans-people. Providing unisex facilities is a cheap response with a profound impact.

If you can't get the hang of the pronouns, try some gender free ones:

sie/ze – (s/he)

hir – (him/her)

hirs – (hers/his)

Mir – (Mr/Ms)

Or try using 'they' as a gender-neutral singular – this is increasingly acceptable in informal contexts. Making an effort to speak the language when you're abroad usually gets results. Finally, remember that the two-sex/gender model is excessively limiting and an inadequate description of reality.

Tale's end

Encountering gender dissidents for the first time can be disturbing and can arouse strong feelings. We can appear incomprehensible or contrary. It may help you to understand we are not doing this for your benefit but for ours, and we use the best tools and knowledge we have. It is likely we have a deeper understanding of sex and gender than you, which is hardly surprising, and we may be quite firm or belligerent about points that appear insignificant. They are not insignificant to us. We have been belaboured by sex and gender our whole lives, and may be desperately carving out a space where we can make sense of ourselves; we may be fighting for our very survival.

The surgical protocols we use are flawed, are premised on breeding but applied to sterile bodies. They are supported by an inflexible model that fails to accommodate reality. But they are the only protocols we have, and produce results. This is unsatisfactory, even though it worked for me; surgical risks for many transsexual procedures are high and expected gains often illusory, surgically constructed genitals often turn out to lack some of the function or appearance that patients hoped for. The aftermath, of gender disorientation, of being in *another* wrong body, can be catastrophic, and terminal. The current protocol is inflexible and flows seamlessly from assessing gender to imposing sex and the gender clinics have an unenviable job navigating a fine line between clinical need and ideology.

Understanding transgender is often about unlearning habits of thought that have taken a lifetime to accumulate, realising that there are no clear answers and making a decision anyway. I hope that one day the screening for surgery becomes more nuanced, widening surgical options, enabling partial transition, creating a socially validated space for viable dissident identities. But that must happen hand in hand with society validating a space. Conversely I would hope a reassessment of gender options does not result in hardship to other trans-people by denying them existing, workable if flawed, solutions; that gender dissidence does not close the door on transsexual transition. But regardless of the risks I firmly believe that this debate needs to be had; for some of us at least, this fairytale must come to an end.

CHAPTER 6

A Queer Kind of Care: Some Preliminary Notes and Observations

Ann Cronin and Andrew King

Introduction

This chapter, drawing on empirical research, examines the experiences of giving and receiving care among older lesbian, gay and bisexual (hereafter LGB) adults.[1] Traditionally, researchers and policy makers tended to assume that all older people experienced later life in a similar way. This can be characterised as the 'normal model of ageing'. However, there has been a growing awareness that this is not the case and that individual and social diversity, for example gender, economic status and ethnicity, may result in older people experiencing later life in very different ways. While this awareness is to be welcomed, little attention has been paid to sexual diversity in later life. Although older LGB adults will have much in common with older heterosexual adults, the way in which sexuality is organised in society means that this group may experience later life differently from their heterosexual counterparts.

Existing research documents the disadvantages faced by older LGB adults while simultaneously dispelling the myth of a lonely old age due to familial and societal rejection. For example, Robinson (1998) indicates that the health care needs of older LGB adults are framed in accordance with stereotypical representations and understandings of their sexuality, while MetLife (2006) and Kurdeck (2005) suggest that care giving and receiving among the older

LGB population differs from the general population in relation to both gender and care practices.

Research that highlights the care needs and practices among older LGB adults is to be welcomed; nevertheless we want to explore some of the difficulties and problems that may arise when the identities of care giver and care receiver are applied to older LGB adults. In order to do this we will be using the concept of heteronormativity, which can help us to think about the relationship between sexuality and society.

Many people consider their sexuality to be a private matter; however we only need to think about the laws, rules, norms and values that surround sexuality in society to realise that, far from being a private matter, sexuality is socially organised and regulated. One way of understanding this is through the concept of heteronormativity, which refers to the organisation of society around the belief that heterosexuality is superior to homosexuality, and the consequent belief that it is only right that society is organised for the benefit of the majority heterosexual population. In this sense heterosexuality is regarded as the dominant mode for conducting intimate relationships, which in turn is linked to traditional cultural beliefs about the way women and men should behave, for example the belief that men are naturally sexually active, while women are naturally sexually passive.

The concept of heteronormativity, referring as it does to the privileging of certain dominant forms of heterosexuality, goes beyond the perhaps more familiar terms of homophobia and heterosexism. The focus is upon inequality and the disadvantages faced by those who are not heterosexual, while also allowing us to consider how these conditions might affect people who are heterosexual. One of the key arguments in this chapter is that both health and social care policy and practice is often underpinned, albeit unwittingly, by heteronormative attitudes and behaviours.

We begin by outlining why there is a need for both policy makers and health and social care practioners to pay more attention to the interaction between gender, sexuality and ageing. Following this we focus on existing literature in this area, paying particular attention to the issues of formal and informal care giving and receiving among older LGB adults. This provides the basis for our critical analysis of the heteronormative assumptions underpinning care and the identity categories on which it is based. We illustrate these with reference to a case study of the caring experiences of two gay men. In conclusion we provide some practical suggestions for the way in which both policy makers and service providers can begin to pay greater attention to the experiences of this cohort of older adults. However, we must recognise that people use categories such as LGB for positive as well as negative effects. Indeed, we are not dismissing them or their importance in the struggle for recognition. We do, nonetheless, think that a thorough consideration of what they encompass is necessary.

Sexuality and ageing: a notable silence

In order to understand the relationship between sexuality and ageing we need to begin by understanding what we mean by the term old age. Far from being a commonsense term, its meaning is socially, culturally and historically dependent (Jamieson, 2002; Posner, 1995). It is for this reason that, as indicated above, traditional models of 'normal ageing' have been challenged by a growing awareness of individual and social diversity. The importance of this awareness should not be underestimated because, as Featherstone and Hepworth (1991) point out, traditional models of old age serve to 'mask' differential experiences. Hence, both Calasanti (1996) and Latimer (1997) have suggested that greater attention needs to be paid to the practices of categorising and how they impact on the delivery of health and social care to older adults as much as any objective understanding of older people. As the following discussion suggests, this may be particularly significant when it comes to considering sexual identity categories.

The growing focus on the many different realities of ageing (Dannefer, 1996) has increased our understanding of gender, class, race/ethnicity and cultural diversity; nevertheless, there has been little mainstream focus on sexual diversity (Cronin, 2004; Heaphy, 2007; Hudspith, 1999). However, it is important to put this absence in a wider context, namely the traditional social policy silence on matters relating to sexuality. For example, sexual health promotion material is in general aimed at young people, the assumption being that older people are not sexually active. While practitioners and academics alike do not necessarily actively endorse the cultural myths surrounding sexuality in later life (cultural myths that both desexualise older people and subject them to ridicule when they are sexual), their silence on the subject has done little to challenge these damaging and inaccurate stereotypes.

Policy into practice

While sexuality is important in later life, it is an issue that is too often overlooked by service providers (Ward *et al.*, 2005). Although this position is slowly beginning to change, an over-emphasis on the physiological aspects of sexuality all too often results in dismissal of the psychological or the sociological. Furthermore, research on service provision (for example Aizenberg *et al.*, 2002; Langley, 2001; Ward *et al.*, 2005) suggests that care workers routinely engage in the control and regulation of sexuality and sexual behaviour among older adults in residential care, with interesting gender differences being apparent. Reinforcing dominant cultural beliefs about gender and sexuality, older men's sexuality is to be controlled through strategies of prevention and regulation while women's sexuality either remains invisible or is actively protected, presumably from the advances of 'deviant' old men. Such research findings suggest that many practitioners and care workers, albeit unwittingly, contribute to reinforcing the dominant cultural myths surrounding sexuality in later life. As Ward *et al.* (2005) note, despite recent reforms to care practice in the UK, which came about as a result of the Care Standards Act (2000), sexuality and ageing are rarely considered, particularly in institutionalised forms of care.

Understanding the relationship between ageing and sexuality

The lack of attention to sexuality is further compounded when it comes to considering the experiences of older LGB identified adults, whose experiences have been relegated to the margins of both policy and service provision (Cronin, 2004; Heaphy, 2007; Price, 2005). While not dismissing the problems associated with measuring populations of sexual minorities, a problem which in this case is further complicated by age (for a discussion see Rosenfeld, 2002 below), Age Concern (2002) estimates that 1 in 15 of its service users will be an LGB adult, thus representing a small but significant minority. Yet as Ward et al (2005, p. 51) state, 'neither in policy nor practice does the older lesbian or gay man exist as a category or a client'. However, as the discussion so far indicates, there is a conundrum in adopting this stance. While at one level we would argue there is a need to raise awareness in service provision through the introduction of identity categories such as 'lesbian' or 'gay man', we would caution against their use in an unproblematic manner, which does not take account of the diversity contained within them. This point is explained in further detail below.

In a study of older LGB adults in the US, Rosenfeld (2002) identifies two 'identity cohorts', which she suggests will impact on later life experiences. The first cohort primarily consisting of the 'old-old', are adults who became aware of their sexuality prior to the Gay Liberation Movement (GLM). Lacking an alternative meaning, many LGB adults, Rosenfeld argues, internalised the dominant cultural understanding of homosexuality as pathological and deviant, leading to the development of poor self-image and low self esteem. Homosexuality in the 1960s was routinely treated with aversion therapy and it was not until 1992 that the World Health Organisation (WHO) declassified homosexuality as a mental disorder. In the UK male homosexuality was not decriminalised until 1967 and then only for adults over the age of 21. Within this hostile climate it was expedient for lesbians and gay men to adopt lifelong survival strategies such as secrecy and 'passing' (in their dealings with officialdom including health and social care services). Despite a liberalisation of laws and changing cultural attitudes towards homosexuality, research suggests (Langley, 2001; Rosenfeld, 2002) that it is likely this group of 'old-old' LGB adults will continue to be strategic in regard to disclosing their sexuality in later life.

Langley's (2001) study of older LGB adults accessing social care demonstrates the active strategies adopted by this group who have an understandable reluctance to 'come out' to service providers. Yet the ability to come out in a supportive and accepting environment would affect the quality of care received. As a result Langley urges social workers in the first instance to become more adept at picking up clues in order to provide an appropriate level of service to this group, while Lee (2007) has highlighted the importance of service providers signalling their recognition of sexual diversity by creating 'gay-friendly' care settings. Such advice implies the need to move beyond the liberal humanitarian approach within social work which often results in 'sexuality blindness', i.e. treating all people the same and not recognising the very real differences that come from being an older LGB adult.

In a more radical stance Harrison (2006) states that institutional heteronormativity present in the care services actively contributes to the invisibility of older LGB adults. Thus it may not simply be a case of old LGB adults continuing with outdated and by implication unnecessary strategies of secrecy and passing; older adults may be justified in their fear that 'coming out' will have a detrimental effect on both the quality of care they receive and their ability to continue to engage in long-term relationships and friendships.

In contrast, Rosenfeld's second 'identity cohort' consists primarily of the 'young-old': women and men who embraced a lesbian or gay identity and lifestyle either during the Gay Liberation Movement or in the period directly following it. This group had access to a self-affirmative and celebratory discourse, thus affecting personal conceptualisations of their sexual identity. This group is more likely to be visible, belong to social networks and communities and lobby for services. Despite the usefulness of Rosenfeld's identity cohorts, they do not address the experiences of women and men who have adopted a non-heterosexual identity and/or lifestyle later in life (Cronin, 2004) and hence may form a third identity cohort, which may cut across age boundaries. Just from this brief discussion it is clear that membership of identity cohorts may affect the experience of care giving and receiving in later life.

Research suggests that compared to their heterosexual counterparts, older LGB adults may have both greater psychological strength to face the difficulties of ageing (Berger and Kelly, 1986; Friend, 1990; Kimmel, 1978) and higher rates of participation in non-familial social networks (Cronin, 2004; Dorfman et al., 1995). Dorfman et al. (1995) show that while older lesbian and gay adults are less likely to receive support from family members than their heterosexual peers, they do receive high levels of social support from friends, leading to the term 'friendship families'. Friend (1990) argues that the achievement of an 'affirmative' lesbian or gay identity encourages the development of psychological strength that can be drawn upon in later life. Kimmel (1978) asserts that successful negotiation of the 'coming out' process and subsequently learning to manage the challenges posed by living in a homophobic society leave an individual with increased 'ego strength'.

However, the existence of only a few visible lesbian and gay areas (e.g. Brighton, Central London, or the Manchester 'Village') in the UK means that the majority of non-heterosexual people live in communities without a visible LGB presence. This may limit the possibility for developing relationships or networks while at the same time it can lead to both feelings and experiences of social isolation (Bell and Valentine, 1995; Valentine, 1993). Likewise, previous research (Cronin, 2004) highlights that geographical location, socio-economic status, life-style choices and age cohort impact upon the level of access and participation in older LGB networks, which may in turn impact on care experiences and access to care in later life. For example, bearing in mind the possible existence of a third identity cohort, Cronin (2004) suggests that older women who did not adopt a lesbian lifestyle until later in life, often following marriage and children, may find it difficult to access and participate in lesbian networks and communities. The major barrier to participation for these women was the lack of a locally based lesbian network and an inability to move to one either because of a lack of financial resources or existing family ties. This situation was particularly acute for women with children still living at home and/or who were not in paid employment. These women found it extremely difficult, if not impossible, to either initiate an intimate relationship or become involved in lesbian and gay networks, with the Internet providing an important access point to lesbian networks.

Such findings both point to the diversity of experience and cast further doubt over the validity of assuming that sexual identity is fixed and unchanging. It is highly likely that this issue will also affect older gay men and as such needs to be taken into consideration in practice. These factors alongside other aspects of identity, including gender, ethnicity and physical ability, must be considered when assessing the care needs of older LGB adults, thus avoiding any assumption that this cohort of older adults are the same, with identical needs or perspectives. This point is paramount when it comes to a consideration of the specific issue of care giving and receiving among older LGB adults.

Care and sexuality: a queer kind of care

We have already noted the absence of an understanding of the relationship between sexuality and ageing in institutional care settings, therefore in this section we focus on the informal care practices of older LGB adults. However before doing so it is useful to define what we mean by the concept of care. As others have noted (Fine, 2005; James, 1992; Thomas, 1993), care covers a broad spectrum of tasks, relationships, contexts and identities; it is a complex set of emotional and embodied phenomena that are subject to change over time.

Drawing on this understanding of care, we note that although practices of care are mentioned within studies of older LGB adults, they have not been a key theme of UK research, an omission that has been acknowledged (Communities Scotland, 2005; Hudspith, 1999; Milne, *et al.*, 2001; Roulstone, *et al.*, 2006). For example, research examining the housing, health and social care provision alongside the general experience of ageing (Heaphy and Yip, 2006; Hubbard and Rossington, 1995; Stonewall Cymru and Triangle Wales, 2006) has indicated that the health care needs of older LGB adults are framed in accordance with stereotypical representations and understandings of their sexuality (Hunt and Minsky, 2005; Robinson, 1998), yet researchers do not go on to further explore actual care practices.

Where research has been conducted, care giving and receiving among the older LGB population differs from the general population in relation to both gender and care practices (Kurdek, 2005; MetLife, 2006). For example, the MetLife study, which surveyed 1000 LGB adults aged between 40 and

61 years of age, indicated higher proportions of gay men providing care to elderly parents than in the heterosexual population, while they were less likely than older lesbians to be caring for adult children. In part, this reflects the heteronormative framework within which care giving and receiving have been theorised and explored in mainstream research on ageing, which, we have suggested, then goes on to influence policy and practice (see Cronin, 2004, for a discussion on this issue). Nevertheless, it does indicate how care practices reflect social divisions. Studies of LGB adults caring also highlight the importance of non-familial relationships – 'families of choice' – and the suggestion that roles of care givers and care receivers may be fluid, interchangeable and context-dependent (Manthorpe and Price, 2005; Northmore *et al.*, 2005). Therefore, simply assuming that age and sexuality are pre-eminent identities affecting someone's experiences of care may be problematic, warranting a different approach to research, policy and the provision of care and support.

A queer kind of care?

While recognising the importance of the aforementioned studies, we are arguing for an approach to care that focuses more on what people do and how they narrate what they do, than with trying to 'fit' them into pre-existing identity categories or roles. To do this, we are drawing on several ideas from the social sciences that in one way or another recognise that people's lives are too complex to categorise simplistically. While practitioners may be well aware of this to some extent, the models and theories that inform their practice may not reflect this complexity. To give an example, rather than suggesting that because someone is gay, lesbian or bisexual they are excluded from care settings or marginalised within them, we are more interested in how a person who identifies themselves as such narrates exclusion and marginalisation, if at all, and how they construct their sense of who they are, their identity, in relation to these experiences. At the same time, we want to consider how the identities that they use affect their understandings of care.

The approaches that we have drawn upon include Queer Theory, Feminist Theory and Narrative Analysis (for discussions of these see Butler, 1999; Earthy and Cronin, 2008; Fuss, 1991; Green, 2007; Riessman, 1993). Without delineating these here, it is important for the reader to recognise what these approaches mean. Overall, they emphasise that who people are, their identities, and what people do, their practices, are socially constructed; that is, social forces, relationships and ideas shape the meanings given to these things. We noted earlier that in our society people construct their sexuality in relation to heteronormativity. What the approaches we are using have in common is that all of them recognise the significance of this and how it shapes the social contexts in which people live their lives.

Our approach therefore explores social contexts or, more precisely, the accounts or stories that people give of their social contexts. By exploring these, we demonstrate how sexual identities and caring are complex, interrelated and liable to transform over time, at both an individual and social level. We can see how these identities and practices are constructed in a wider biographical and social perspective. To outline this in more detail, we will sketch out the lives of two older gay men, Alec and Peter.

CASE STUDY – ALEC

Alec is sixty-four years old and has had diabetes for most of his adult life. Peter is a fifty-five year old nurse. Alec and Peter have been friends and lived together for over twenty-five years, although both have also had long-term partners. This could be viewed as an example of a 'family of choice' noted earlier, although when examining their narratives the issue of choice appears more complex. Indeed, although they are not a couple in the traditional sense (i.e. have never been sexual partners), their lives are very much intertwined.

When Alec and Peter first met, Alec's diabetes had become erratic and he was ill on a regular basis. Although Peter did not work as a nurse at the time, he supported Alec physically, emotionally and financially. For instance, he took control, making Alec visit various private doctors and specialists, obtaining better care for him, until his condition was stabilised; he nursed him when he was particularly ill; he helped him cope with the psychological stress of his chronic illness; and when Alec had to retire early on health grounds, Peter continued to support him financially. It could be assumed, therefore, that Peter has for many years taken the role and identity of being Alec's carer. However, when examining their stories in more detail and enquiring about changes in their lives and their current situation, a different, more complex representation is revealed, a representation that locates the care practices noted above within their understandings and feelings about their sexuality, about ageing and about the heteronormative society in which they have lived.

When they first met, Peter was struggling to come to terms with his sexuality. Although their adult lives have been lived after the 1967 Act, when the age of consent for homosexuals was set at 21 years of age, both men had grown up and been socialised in a more homophobic climate. Peter felt that his family, and in particular his father, did not understand his sexuality and would not accept it. This caused him considerable psychological distress, to the extent that he was advised by his GP to seek help. It was at this point in his life that he met Alec at a local lesbian and gay support network. Alec helped Peter to accept his sexuality and viewed from this perspective he can be seen as caring for Peter psychologically, while Peter tried to support Alec with his diabetes.

In recent years, Alec has suffered from further ill health and Peter, although continuing to work, has also suffered periods of illness. Again, we can see a complex set of practices relating to support, care and interdependence. Peter is learning to cope with Alec's increasing infirmity, while Alec faces coping with Peter's growing depressions and frustrations. Alec fears Peter will grow tired of caring for him and leave, while Peter is concerned he will not be able to cope, both physically and psychologically, with Alec as he ages; in effect, he needs care himself and is not sure if Alec can provide it.

What can Alec and Peter's story tell us about older LGB adults and caring? First, Peter and Alec do not simply perform pre-existing roles. Both are carer and both are cared for. So care giving and receiving are not fixed or determined roles, they are a mixture of practices both men undertake at different points, in different contexts (see Forbat, 2005, for further discussion of how the roles of 'carer' and 'caree' intermix). Any policy models that identify care giving and care receiving as identity roles are thus problematic. Certainly, Alec and Peter do not fit this type of model and practitioners would need to view these men according to what they are doing, not according to pre-specified expectations.

Second, Alec and Peter's care practices are embedded in their identities as gay men: they care for each other partly because their sexuality brought them together and because of the lives that they have carved for themselves. This is in accordance with research we noted earlier, concerning the importance of social networks (Dorfman *et al.*, 1995). However, because they identify themselves as gay men and because they are not in a sexual relationship, their care practices transgress domestic and emotional norms related to gender and care, which, as we noted earlier, are largely heteronormative and often taken for granted. Neither man is the other's partner; both are involved in caring for each other in different ways. There are no legal or conjugal obligations to care. For practitioners, Alec and Peter demonstrate the complexity of negotiating care relationships and the understandings that we bring to them.

Third, it may appear that Alec and Peter have chosen to care for each other. However, we must consider to what extent this so-called choice is actually a choice at all. Alec and Peter's choices have been and continue to be shaped by the heteronormative society in which they have grown up and grown old. Their personal experience of society and of homophobia has shaped what they do and how they do it. They may well have certain psychological strengths (Friend, 1990; Kimmel, 1978), although their narratives suggest choices and decisions made in an ad hoc manner, often in the face of discrimination and adversity: a local 'fix' to a social problem. Again, this raises issues about how service providers can best serve those who may be highly self-sufficient because of their experiences.

Practices of possibility

In view of the points we have made in relation to Alec and Peter, policy makers, service providers and practitioners in health and social care may wish to consider several points. First, taking seriously the narratives of LGB adults means reconsidering (indeed reconfiguring) the purpose of fixed identity categories, both in academic and practitioner-oriented texts and in everyday life. We cannot just assume that older LGB adults will identify themselves as such in care settings or when undertaking care.

Similarly, we should not assume that their reasons for not identifying themselves as LGB are marginalisation or exclusion. As we have demonstrated, older LGB adults, to use the category for explanatory purposes, are diverse; the practices of caring that they employ are similarly diverse and contextualised. Therefore, we would suggest that rather than viewing older LGB adults as an additional group for practitioners to engage with, their experiences could teach us much about care per se. In other words, practitioners and others should not look at the care experiences of older LGB adults as somehow distinct, but think about what they can imply for all older adults, whatever their sexual orient-ation. Coping with inequalities of power, of access to healthcare, of stigma, and developing mechanisms to become empowered are issues that affect all.

While we are arguing for a more thorough analysis of the lives of older LGB adults, we do not wish to marginalise or categorise this broad group further. As we stated at the beginning of this chapter, it is essential to recognise the categories that people hold important in their everyday lives. This places practitioners in something of a dilemma. As we call for the 'queering' or problematising of these categories, this does not mean that we would suggest that health care practitioners deny them or try to gather all people who do not identify themselves as heterosexual under the umbrella of queer. Instead, we hope to have demonstrated that focusing on how people use these categories and describe their practices as care are just as significant.

Given the above, it is important to consider some points that have been made by others. Langley (2001), for instance, argues that there needs to be an awareness and sensitivity that many older LGB adults may actively seek to hide their sexuality from service providers, social workers and such like. Hence, there is a need for practitioners to be sensitive to clues regarding sexuality, and then find ways to validate relationships and lifestyles. This is imperative. As we explained, research has shown that many older LGB adults may not access health and social care due to a fear of hostility. This may have particular implications when practitioners come to assess informal care work practices, thus increasing the burdens on all.

Finally, there must also be a willingness to challenge heteronormative assumptions about sexuality and especially sexuality in later life. Thus there must be a cultural shift in the willingness of organisations and service providers to address these issues. Appropriate services for older LGB adults need to be developed; this might be within mainstream provision, or it might include the setting up of an older LGB group. Some organisations have already achieved this, but again we would caution against viewing these as examples of 'doing enough' or claiming to recognise diversity. As we have suggested, older LGB adults may not wish to be identified in certain care settings or other health and social care contexts.

Conclusion

In this chapter we have presented health and social care practitioners with some of the issues related to the use of identity categories when examining the care practices of older LGB adults. We began by noting that the lives of these adults have often been ignored by research on ageing and later life that informs policy initiatives and models of care. However, we have also noted that when older LGB adults' lives have been studied there are similarities to and differences from their heterosexual peers. We have explained that this is due, in part, to the heteronormative framework that underlies our society and shapes how older LGB adults' identities are viewed by themselves and others, together with the care practices that they employ. Recounting the story of Alec and Peter, we have illustrated the complexity, diversity and contextual nature of sexuality and care.

No two LGB adults will experience their sexuality in the same way; likewise, how this shapes the way they care and whom they care for will be similarly diverse. We recognise that this places practitioners in something of a dilemma, as it does us as researchers. However, we believe that recognising diversity as something that is lived, as experienced in daily life, not just as a policy agenda or initiative, means accepting and engaging with people as humans not simply as categories. Furthermore, it means questioning the nature of these categories at all levels, in all situations.

Note

1. Although the experiences of older transgender adults are likely to overlap in some ways with the experiences of older LGB adults, there will also be many differences, differences that we are unable to do justice to in a chapter of this size. Therefore, while not dismissing the need to look at the experience of older transgender adults, our discussion here is limited to the experience of older LGB adults.

CHAPTER 7

Conclusion

Richard Ward and Rebecca L. Jones

In this concluding section we review the findings and messages from the different chapters and consider how they might assist readers to think in a more critical and questioning fashion about the topics covered. We start by discussing further the three main approaches to categories that we introduced at the beginning of the book. We then summarise the argument that has built throughout the book that simply remembering that some people are LGBT[1] is insufficient. We recap the ways in which heteronormativity means that profound problems of exclusion and invisibility remain unaddressed. We then argue that the task of reframing care practices in the light of dissident sexual and gender identities is further complicated by the complex and variable nature of these categories. We summarise what the chapters have shown about the ways in which these categories are troubled, before moving on to argue for the need to place sexuality and gender in context.

Revisiting approaches

In the Introduction we introduced three distinctive ways of thinking about sexual and gender identity categories – person-centred approaches, rights-based approaches and deconstructive approaches. In this concluding chapter we do not recommend one approach over the others, but draw out the relationship between approaches and underlying theorisations of identities. We also suggest a fruitful way of dealing with these different approaches in everyday practice.

What, then, are the implications of using the three different approaches in terms of what status they give to sexual and gender identity labels?

Person-centred approaches to sexual and gender identities may use labels such as 'lesbian', 'dyke', 'queer' or 'homosexual', or they may not. Whether these categories are used or not will depend on individual service users' preferences. In this way, person-centred approaches do not depend on any particular underlying theory of the nature of sexual and gender identities – they provide a way of working, rather than a specific understanding of these sorts of categories. Rights-based approaches do usually use such labels, and have historically tended to treat such identities as relatively fixed and essential. However, this does not have to be the case – these identities can be thought of as beneficial in particular situations but not 'real', as we discuss further below. The deconstructive approach entails conceptualising such identities as fluid, variable and context-dependent, that is, viewing them as socially constructed rather than biological or essential. This may better reflect the variability of people's lives and experiences and it enables the wider histori-cal and cultural context to be taken into account, as the chapters in this book have demonstrated.

One useful way of working with these different approaches to sexual and gender identities is by using Weeks's concept of 'necessary fictions' (Weeks, 1995). Dissident sexual (and, we would add, gender) identities are necessary because they help create a collective sense of belonging that has at times proved crucial to the lives and interests of LGBT people. Such categories can represent a common interest and provide a banner under which to unite. But these same categories are also fictions, argues Weeks, because they are never able to fully convey the lived experience of sexuality. They are products of their time or 'historical inventions'. Thus practitioners should give careful attention to using the right labels for a particular situation, while also recognising that all such labels are provisional and imperfectly reflect the complexities of people's lives. In some situations it may be appropriate to use identity categories as if they were relatively fixed and stable, in others it may not. We would argue that all three approaches to gender and sexual identity can be used in ways that respect the diversity and variability of people's experiences.

Recognising heteronormativity

Having explored the implications of the different approaches to gender and sexual identity categories, we turn now to a necessary first step in improving care services – recognising the ways in which exclusion and discrimination occur through heteronormativity. While there are many ways in which LBGT people are overtly discriminated against, such as the examples given by the older lesbians who took part in Archibald's study, subtler forms of exclusion are perhaps more insidious and difficult to counter. The concept of heteronormativity (Warner, 1991) goes beyond the more straightforward notions of discrimination suggested by the use of terms such as 'heterosexism' or 'homophobia' (for discussion of the distinctions between these two terms, see Fish, 2006). It directs our attention to the ways heterosexuality is privileged and taken as the standpoint from which everything else is judged.

As Cronin and King underline in their discussion of care, tackling heteronormativity means challenging the way that heterosexuality is made to appear 'natural' and 'normal', and everything else second best. Sexuality is often only 'seen' or made explicit when it refers to homosexuality or bisexuality. Rarely is heterosexuality thought about or treated as a sexual category in the same way, as MacKian and Goldring discuss in relation to health promotion. Likewise, the existence of two separate and distinct genders is usually taken entirely for granted, despite the body of evidence that both gender and sex are more of a continuum, as Alleyn and Jones overview.

Cronin and King demonstrate some of the ways that starting from the experience of non-heterosexual people can shed light on other care categories such as 'care-giver' and 'care'. Such categories may be as unhelpful to heterosexual service users as to LGBT ones (Forbat, 2005). Not taking traditional heterosexual lifestyles and care roles for granted can carry benefits for everyone involved in care.

Being aware of the concept of heteronormativity also helps practitioners to recognise the ways in which sexual and gender identities are enforced and policed by care practices themselves. As Alleyn and Jones demonstrate, medicine is still a key player in the ongoing process of shaping trans identities – trans people have to conform to a particular version of gender identity in order to get treatment. Similarly, Jones includes a case study where a service user's right to access a bereavement service depended on her drawing on a particular identity. Individuals do not choose their sexual and gender identity freely but always within a political and social context that privileges particular types of identities, usually traditional heterosexual ones.

As other commentators have also argued (Hicks 2008; Hicks and Watson, 2003; Fish, 2008), LGBT issues cannot simply be added in to existing patterns of provision if the goal is to develop truly inclusive care services and practices. The culture of health and social care as a whole needs to be critically examined to identify and address the ways in which it is heteronormative.

Troubling categories

The task of rethinking care services and practices is further complicated by the fluid and variable nature of sexual and gender identities, which has been the main focus of this book. Each chapter has provided examples of ways in which 'standard' dissident identities such as 'lesbian', 'gay', 'bisexual' and 'transsexual' can be inadequately reflective of people's experiences and identity preferences. The authors have argued for the need constantly to bear in mind how categories are being applied, what assumptions accompany them and what limitations and exclusions are involved.

The authors have demonstrated some of the inadequacies of a view of sexuality and gender as 'fixed' and determined by biology and physiology. Furthermore, Jones in Chapter 4 and Alleyn and Jones in Chapter 5 have demonstrated some of the problems arising from a belief that individuals are either heterosexual or gay/lesbian and male or female, respectively. As Jones illustrates in her discussion of bisexuality, individuals who cannot be located in this either/or model of gay or straight sexual identity often meet with hostility and disbelief because they pose a threat to the ways we commonly understand sexuality. Similarly, the dissident trans perspective that Alleyn and Jones outline, which rejects a wholly masculine or feminine identity, challenges a largely unquestioned either/or model of gender and biological sex. As these authors demonstrate, it is often through this process of troubling categories that we are made to rethink existing approaches to sexuality and gender and the assumptions that underpin them.

Accompanying the either/or model of sexuality and gender is often the belief that identity categories are fixed and stable. A common understanding is that we inhabit a certain sexual or gender identity throughout our lives. Such an assumption is questioned by this book, through a focus on ageing and the lifecourse, as we discuss in more detail in the next section. The biographical narratives and case studies contained here (see especially Jones, MacKian and Goldring, and Cronin and King) reveal the ways in which sexuality is negotiated and evolving and might usefully be thought of more as a process than as a fixed attribute, both historically and biographically. The meanings attached to sexual and gender categories in society at any given time, coupled with the conditions under which we live and the opportunities we have for self-expression and definition, all influence what categories are brought into play.

A key message of this book is the importance of supporting individuals in defining and redefining their own identities rather than imposing categories upon them. Alleyn and Jones underline the vital importance of paying attention to people's own terminology to describe their gender identity. Without this attention to individual identity people may end up pushed further along a continuum of a particular gender than they want to be, a particularly serious issue if this entails irreversible surgery. As Jones outlines in relation to bisexuality, although the point is more generally applicable, there are important distinctions to be made between how a person feels, how they behave and which identities they subscribe to. People may, for instance, engage in same-sex activity but not consider themselves to be gay, lesbian or bisexual. As MacKian and Goldring illustrate in relation to health promotion, in order to effectively engage people there is always a need to begin by asking how people define themselves. Taking the time to find out someone's preferred identity label (if they have one at all) vastly increases practitioners' ability to provide sensitive and appropriate services.

Another common assumption that is questioned by the authors contributing to this book is that categories of identity are homogenous and coherent. In other words, each person subscribing to a particular sexual or gender category shares the same characteristics as others who identify in a similar way. Based upon this view it is often argued that homosexuality, bisexuality and transsexuality are knowable and can be broken down into a series of features or attributes that enables health and social care practitioners to predict the needs of LGBT service users without getting to know them at an individual level. MacKian and Goldring challenge the logic of this as they unpick the presumptions behind a 'one size fits all' approach to health promotion and the gay community. Generational differences are shown to shape the way that gay men make sense of their sexuality and their participation in a commercial scene, consequently requiring a more nuanced approach from service providers. Similarly, as Alleyn and Jones illustrate in respect to the trans community, there is a diverse range of approaches to gender identity that include various choices about surgery and different degrees of transitioning from one gender category to another.

Any effort to make a claim for what defines and unites a particular group almost inevitably leads to exclusions and to the silencing of certain voices. One of the challenges to practitioners is to think about sexuality and gender identity in ways that are inclusive and that allow contrasts and dissent. This is also the case for practitioners who themselves identify as LGBT when the temptation may be to assume that someone using the same identity label means the same things by it. An over-arching message is that people 'do' sexuality and gender differently from one another.

Lives in context

We have argued throughout this book for the need to place sexuality and gender in context. In particular, we have placed emphasis upon ageing and the lifecourse as a means to demonstrate the changing and negotiated quality of sexual and gender identities. The chapters in this book have given particular prominence to the process of time – time at an individual biographical level, but also at a wider level of social and historical change. By thinking about sexuality and gender 'in time' we are better able to understand that it is an open-ended and fluid aspect of identity, an issue we now examine in more detail.

One way in which sexuality and gender in time has been addressed is through an exploration of generational differences offered by MacKian and Goldring. The authors show that a generational framework is directly applicable to health and social care in terms of understanding the interplay of biographical narratives and wider social change. So, for many older gay men who will have first-hand experience of a time when homosexuality was criminalised and pathologised, there is a need to consider how this experience shapes their view of health and social care in the present. A person's age and the climate in which they grew up can have a crucial bearing upon how they negotiate their sexuality and gender in the present, including their approach to accessing health and social care services.

Another key consideration is how self-definition alters over time. Changes in self-definition over time are, of course, fundamental to trans identities – trans people have made some movement in their gender identity over the course of their lives. In relation to sexuality, Jones offers a case study of a woman in her late 70s who has identified in different ways at various points in her life. This had an influence upon the network of support that she was able to draw upon at different stages of her life. Similarly, both Archibald's and Cronin and King's chapters highlight that the point in her life at which a woman first identifies as lesbian can have a crucial impact upon the networks of support that exist for her in later life. Sexuality is thereby very much integral to the ageing process while our age shapes the way we 'do' sexuality.

Both Eaglesham in Chapter 1 and Alleyn and Jones in Chapter 5 draw upon historical change to illustrate the ways in which sexuality and gender identity have been subject to an ongoing process of redefinition and reconstruction. Both chapters reveal the role played by social institutions, including the Welfare State, in influencing how sexuality and gender is understood.

Closing comments

Overall, this book has outlined the way in which everyday practices and beliefs contribute to the construction of dissident sexuality and gender. Very often it is the most routine and day-to-day patterns of working that maintain assumptions about what is normal or natural. As the authors contributing to this book highlight, there is a need to reflect on how health and social care is heterosexualised through these largely unquestioned practices and how best to change this. Ultimately, the agenda for health and social care is not merely to understand and add in dissident sexual and gender identity categories. Rather it is to recognise the complexity of all sexual and gender identities, including heterosexual and traditionally gendered ones, and to use that more nuanced understanding of their nature to challenge heteronormativity and the inequalities based on sexuality and gender identity that stem from it. Only once these inequalities are made visible and addressed will it be possible to develop care services that are truly inclusive and appropriate for everyone.

Note

1. We are aware of the irony of continuing to use the term 'LGBT', an identity category, while attempting to problematise identity categories. We give 'LGBT' no special status above other useful but necessarily meaning-laden umbrella terms, such as 'queer', 'dissident' or 'non-heterosexual'.

References

Adams, M. (2003) 'The reflexive self and culture: a critique', *British Journal of Sociology*, Vol. 54, No. 2, pp. 221–38

Age Concern (2002) 'Issues facing older lesbians, gay men and bisexuals' (online). Available from URL: www.ageconcern.org.uk/AgeConcern/Documents/OLGMppp. pdf (accessed 4 April 2008)

Aizenberg, D., Weizman, A. and Barak, Y. (2002) 'Attitudes towards sexuality among nursing home residents', *Sexuality and Disability*, Vol. 20, No. 3, pp. 185–9.

Anderlini-D'Onofrio, S. (ed.) (2004) *Plural Loves: Designs For Bi and Poly Living*, Binghamton: Harrington Park Press

Angelides, S. (2001) *A History of Bisexuality*, Chicago: University of Chicago Press

Arber, S. and Ginn, J. (1994) 'Women and aging', *Reviews in Clinical Gerontology*, Vol.4, No. 4, pp. 349–58

Arber, S. and Ginn, J. (eds) (1995) *Connecting Gender and Ageing: A Sociological Approach*, Buckingham: Open University Press

Arber, S., Davidson, K. and Ginn, J. (eds) (2003) *Gender and Ageing: Changing Roles and Relationships*, Buckingham: Open University Press

Archibald, C. (2002) '*Half of Them are Dying on Their Feet but They Still Have Strength for That' Sexuality, Dementia and Residential Care Work: a Disregarded and Neglected Area of Study*, PhD thesis, University of Stirling.

Archibald, C. (2005) *Sexuality and Dementia: A Guide for All People Working with People with Dementia*, Stirling University: Dementia Services Development Centre

Armstrong, E. (1995) 'Traitors to the cause? Understanding the lesbian/gay "bisexuality debates"', in Tucker, N. (ed.) (1995) *Bisexual Politics: Theories, Queries, and Visions*, New York: The Haworth Press, pp.199–218

Aronson, J. (1998) 'Lesbians giving and receiving care: stretching conceptualizations of caring and community', *Women's Studies International Forum*, Vol. 21, No. 5, pp. 505–19

Atkinson, P. and Hammersley, M. (1994) 'Ethnography and participant observation', in Denzin, N. and Lincoln, Y. (eds) (1994) *Handbook of Qualitative Research*, Thousand Oaks: Sage, pp. 249–61

Avert (2008) 'Averting HIV and AIDS worldwide' (online). Available from URL: www. avert.org/hsexu3.htm (accessed 22 August 2008)

Bailey, J. V., Farquhar, C., Owen, C. and Whittaker, D. (2003) 'Sexual behaviour of lesbians and bisexual women', *Sexually Transmitted Infection*, Vol. 79, No. 2, pp. 147–50

Balsam, K. F., Beauchaine, T. P., Mickey, R. M. and Rothblum, E. D. (2005) 'Mental health of lesbian, gay, bisexual, and heterosexual siblings: effects of gender, sexual orientation, and family', *Journal of Abnormal Psychology*, Vol. 114, No. 3, pp. 471–6

Barker, M., Bowes-Catton, H., Iantaffi, A., Cassidy, A. and Brewer, L. (2008) 'British bisexuality: a snapshot of bisexual identities in the UK', *Journal of Bisexuality*, Vol. 8, No. 1–2, pp. 141–62

Barker, M., Iantaffi, A. and Gupta, C. (2006) 'Bisexuality research questioned', *Psychologist*, Vol. 19, No. 2, p. 81

Barrett, J. (2007) *Transsexual and other Disorders of Gender Identity*, Oxford: Radcliffe Publishing Ltd

Barrett, J. (2008) personal communication (received 15 October 2008)

Beck, U. (1994) 'The reinvention of politics: towards a theory of reflexive modernization', in Beck, U., Giddens, A. and Lash, S. (eds) (1998) *Reflexive Modernization: Politics, Tradition and Aesthetics in the Modern Social Order*, Cambridge: Polity Press, pp. 1–55

Beeler, J. A., Rawls, T. W., Herdt, G. and Cohler, B. (1999) 'The needs of older lesbians and gay men in Chicago', *Journal of Gay and Lesbian Social Services*, Vol. 9, no. 1, pp. 31–49

Bell, D. and Valentine, G. (eds) (1995) *Mapping Desire: Geographies of Sexualities*, London: Routledge

Bell, L. and Morgan, L. (2003) *First Out*, Stonewall, pp. 1-88 (online). Available from URL: www.stonewall.org.uk/beyond_barriers/information/794.asp (accessed 12 June 2009)

Bellaby, P., Goldring, J. E. and MacKian, S. (2007) *Health Literacy and the Framing of Health Messages in the Gay Community*, ESRC End of Award Report, RES-000-22-1486 Swindon: ESRC

Berger, R. M. and Kelly, J. (1986), 'Working with homosexuals of the older population', *Social Casework*, Vol. 17, April, pp. 203–10

Berkman, C. S. and Zinberg, G. (1997) 'Homophobia and heterosexism in social workers', *Social Work*, Vol. 42, No. 2, pp. 319–32

Bernard, M. (1998) 'Backs to the future? Reflections on women, ageing and nursing', *Journal of Advanced Nursing*, Vol. 27, no. 3, pp. 633–40

Beyond Barriers, Stonewall Project 2002 (online) Available from URL: www.stonewall. org.uk/beyond_barriers/information/multiple_discrimination/807.asp (accessed 12 June 2009)

BiCon UK, www.bicon.org.uk

Binnie, J. and Skeggs, B. (2004) 'Cosmopolitan knowledge and the production and consumption of sexualized space: Manchester's gay village', *Sociological Review*, Vol. 52, No. 1, pp. 39–61

Bloom, A. (2002) *Normal; Transsexual CEOs, Crossdressing Cops, and Hermaphrodites with Attitude*, London: Bloomsbury

Bornstein, K. (1995). *Gender Outlaw: On Men, Women, and the Rest of Us*, New York: Vintage Books

Bowes-Catton, H. (2007) 'Resisting the binary: discourses of identity and diversity in bisexual politics 1988–1996', *Lesbian and Gay Psychology Review*, Vol. 8, No. 1, pp. 58–70

Brotman, S., Ryan, B. and Cormier, R. (2003) 'The health and social service needs of gay and lesbian elders and their families in Canada', *The Gerontologist*, Vol. 43, no. 2, pp. 192–202

Bullough, V. L. and Bullough, B. (1993) *Cross Dressing, Sex, and Gender*, Philadelphia: University of Pennsylvania Press

Burtney, L. and Hosie, A. (2007) *HIV and Sexual Health Promotion Activities for Gay and Bisexual Men and Black and Minority Ethnic/African Communities in Scotland*, HIV Scotland

Butler, J. (1993) *Bodies that Matter: On the Discursive Limits of 'Sex'*, London: Routledge

Butler, J. (1999) *Gender Trouble,* London: Routledge

Byron Smith, G. (1993) 'Homophobia and attitudes toward gay men and lesbians by psychiatric nurses', *Archives of Psychiatric Nursing*, Vol. 7, No. 6, pp. 377–84

Bywater, J. and Jones, R. (2007) *Sexuality in Social Work,* Exeter: Learning Matters

Calasanti, T. M. (1996) 'Incorporating diversity: meaning, levels of research, and implications for theory ', *The Gerontologist*, Vol. 36, No. 2, pp. 147–56

Cant, B. (ed.) (2008) *Footsteps and Witnesses: Lesbian and Gay Lifestories from Scotland*, Edinburgh: Word Power Books

Carr, C. L. (2006) 'Bisexuality as a category in social research: lessons from women's gendered narratives', *Journal of Bisexuality*, Vol. 6, No.4, pp. 29–46

Carr, S., Scoular, A., Elliot, L., Ilett, R. and Meager, M. (1999) 'A community-based lesbian sexual health service: clinically justified or politically correct?' *British Journal of Family Planning*, Vol. 25, No. 3, pp. 93–5

Cayton, H. (2006) 'The flat-pack patient? Creating health together', *Patient Education and Counseling*, Vol. 62, pp. 288–90

Cohen, H. L., Curry, L. C., Jenkins, D., Walker, C. A. and Hogstel, M. O. (2008) 'Older lesbians and gay men: long-term care issues', *Annals of Long Term Care*, Vol. 16 (online). Available from URL: www.annalsoflongtermcare.com/article/8315 (accessed 10 December 2008)

Coia, N., John, S., Dobbie, F., Bruce, S., McGranachan, M. and Simons, L. (2002) *'Something To Tell You': a health needs assessment of young gay, lesbian and bisexual people in Glasgow,* Glasgow: Greater Glasgow NHS Board

Communities Scotland (2005) *Precis No. 67: Housing and support needs of older lesbian, gay, bisexual and transgender (LGBT) people in Scotland*, Edinburgh: Communities Scotland. Available from URL: www.communitiesscotland.gov.uk/stellent/groups/public/documents/webpages/pubcs_008930.pdf (accessed 4 February 2008)

Connell, J. and Hart, G. (2003) 'An Overview of Male Sex Work in Edinburgh and Glasgow: The Male Sex Worker Perspective', Occasional Paper No.8, MRC Social and Public Health Sciences Unit, Glasgow University

Conner, M. and Norman, P. (eds) (1996) *Predicting Health Behaviour: Research and Practice with Social Cognition Models,* Buckingham: Open University Press

Conner, R. P., Sparks, D. H. and Sparks, M. (1997) *Cassell's Encyclopedia of Queer Myth, Symbol and Spirit: Gay, Lesbian, Bisexual and Transgender Lore*, London: Cassell

Copper, B. (1988) *Over the Hill: Reflections on Ageism Between Women,* Freedom, CA: Crossing Press

Cronin, A. (2004) 'Sexuality in gerontology: a heteronormative presence, a queer absence', in Daatland, S. O. and Biggs, S. (eds) (2004) *Ageing and Diversity: Multiple Pathways and Cultural Migrations*, London: Sage, pp.107–22

Dannefer, D. (1996), 'The social organization of diversity, and the normative organization of age', *The Gerontologist*, Vol. 36, No. 2, pp. 174–7

Department for Education and Employment (1999) *A Guide to the Sex Discrimination (Gender Reassignment) Regulations 1999,* HMSO (online). Available from URL: www.pfc.org.uk/node/235 (accessed 22 August 2008)

Department of Health (2001) National Service Framework for Older People, London: Department of Health

Department of Health (2007) *Human Fertilisation and Embryology Bill* (online). Available from URL: www.dh.gov.uk/en/Publicationsandstatistics/Legislation/Actsandbills/DH_080211 (accessed 22 August 2008)

Diamond, L. M. (1998) 'Development of sexual orientation among adolescent and young adult women', *Developmental Psychology*, Vol. 34, No. 5, pp. 1085–95

Dobinson, C., MacDonnell, J., Hampson, E., Clipsham, J. and Chow, K. (2005) 'Improving the access and quality of public health services for bisexuals', *Journal of Bisexuality*, Vol. 5, No. 1, pp. 41–78

Dodge, B. and Sandfort, T. G. M. (2007) 'A review of mental health research on bisexual individuals when compared to homosexual and heterosexual individuals', in Firestein, B. (ed.) (2007) *Becoming Visible: Counseling Bisexuals Across the Lifespan*, New York: Columbia University Press

Donovan, C., Heaphy, B. and Weeks, J. (2001) *Same Sex Intimacies: Families of Choice and Other Life Experiments*, London: Routledge

Dorfman, R., Walters, K., Burke, P., Hardin, L., Karanik, T., Raphael, J. and Silverstein, E. (1995) 'Old, sad and alone: The myth of the aging homosexual', *Journal of Gerontological Social Work*, Vol. 24, No. 1/2, pp. 29–44

Earthy, S. and Cronin, A. (2008) 'Narrative analysis', in Gilbert, N. (ed.) (2008) *Researching Social Life (Third Edition)*, London: Sage, pp. 420–39

Eliade, M. (2004). *Shamanism; Archaic Techniques of Ecstasy*, Princeton: Princeton University Press

Ellis, S. J. (2007) 'Community in the 21st century: issues arising from a current study of British lesbians and gay men', *Journal of Gay and Lesbian Psychotherapy*, Vol. 11, No. 1, pp. 111–26

Epstein, S. (1987) 'Gay politics, ethnic identity: the limits of social constructionism', *Socialist Review*, Vol. 93/94, May–August, pp. 9–54

Equality Network (2000) 'Briefing on the repeal of section 2A/28' (online). Available from URL: www.equality-network.org/Equality/website.nsf/webpages/D1FA211313 05B18F80256FC100576DBD (accessed 25 June 2009)

Equality Network (2008) www.equality-network.org

Evers, H. (1981) 'Care or custody? The experience of women in long stay geriatric wards', in Hutter, B. and Williams, G. (eds) *Controlling Women*, London: Croon Helm

Fausto-Sterling, A. (2000) *Sexing the Body: Gender Politics and the Construction of Sexuality*, New York: Basic Books

Featherstone, M. and Hepworth, M. (1991) 'The mask of ageing and the Postmodern life course', in Featherstone, M., Hepworth, M. and Turner, B. S. (eds) (1991) *The Body: Social Process and Cultural Theory*, London: Sage, pp. 371–89

Feinberg, L. (1996) *Transgender Warriors: Making History from Joan of Arc to Dennis Rodman*, Boston: Beacon Press

Fine, M. (2005) 'Individualisation, risk and the body', *Journal of Sociology*, Vol. 41, No. 3, pp. 247–66

Firestein, B. (ed.) (2007) *Becoming Visible: Counseling Bisexuals Across the Lifespan*, New York: Columbia University Press

Fish, J. (2006) *Heterosexism in Health and Social Care*, Palgrave Macmillan: Basingstoke and New York

Fish, J. (2007) *Reducing Health Inequalities for Lesbian, Gay, Bisexual and Trans People – Briefings for Health and Social Care Staff*, London: Department of Health

Fish, J. (2008) 'Far from mundane: Theorising heterosexism for social work education', *Social Work Education*, Vol. 27, No. 2, pp. 182–193

Forbat, L. (2005) *Talking About Care: Two Sides to the Story*, Bristol: Policy Press

Friend, R. (1990) 'Older lesbians and gay people: a theory of successful aging', *Journal of Homosexuality*, Vol. 20, No. 3–4, pp. 99–117

Fullmer, E., Shenk, D. and Eastland, L. (1999) 'Negating identity: a feminist analysis of the social invisibility of older lesbians', *Journal of Women and Aging*, Vol. 11, No. 2/3, pp. 131–48

Furedi, F. (2007) 'The only thing we have to fear is the 'culture of fear' itself' (online). Available from URL: www.spiked-online.com/index.php?/site/article/3053/ (accessed 11 October 2007)

Fuss, D. (1991) 'Inside/Out', in Fuss, D. (ed.) (1991) *Inside/Out: Lesbian Theories, Gay Theories*, London: Routledge, pp. 1–10

Fyfe, A., Fleming, R. and Reid, S. (2006) *Sexual Orientation Research Phase 3 – A Stocktake of Local Authority Policy and Practice*, Social Research Findings, London: National Centre for Social Research

George, S. (1993) *Women and Bisexuality*, London: Scarlet Press

Giddens, A. (1991) *Modernity and Self Identity*, Stanford: Stanford University Press

Gott, M. (2004) *Sexuality, Sexual Health and Ageing (Rethinking Ageing)*, Maidenhead: Open University Press

Green, A. I. (2007) 'Queer theory and sociology: locating the subject and the self in sexuality studies', *Sociological Theory*, Vol. 25, No. 1, pp. 26–45

Green, R. (1999) *Reflections on 'Transsexualism and Sex Reassignment' 1969–1999: Presidential Address* (online) Available from *International Journal of Transgenderism*, URL: www.symposion.com/ijt/greenpresidential/green00.htm (accessed 8 April 2006)

Griggs, C. (1998) *S/He: Changing Sex and Changing Clothes*, Oxford: Berg

Harding, R., Bensley, J. and Corrigan, N. (2004) 'Targeting smoking cessation to high prevalence communities: outcomes from a pilot intervention for gay men', *BMC Public Health*, Vol. 4, No. 43, pp. 1–5

Haritaworn, J., Lin, C. and Klesse, C. (2006) Special Issue on Polyamory, *Sexualities*, Vol. 9, No. 5, pp. 515–656

Harrison, J. (2006) 'Coming out ready or not! Gay, lesbian, bisexual, transgender and intersex ageing and aged care in Australia: reflections, contemporary developments and the road ahead', *Gay & Lesbian Issues and Psychology Review*, Vol. 2, No. 2, pp. 44–53

Hart, G. J. and Williamson, L. M. (2005) 'Increase in HIV sexual risk behaviour in homosexual men in Scotland, 1996–2002: prevention failure?' *Sexually Transmitted Infections*, Vol. 81, No. 5, pp. 367–72

Hart, G., Williamson, L. and Flowers, P. (2004) 'Good in parts: the Gay Men's Task Force in Glasgow – a response to Kelly', *AIDS Care*, Vol.16, no. 2, pp. 159–65

Hartman, J. E. (2005) 'Another kind of 'chilly climate': the effects of lesbian separatism on bisexual women's identity and community', *Journal of Bisexuality*, Vol. 5, No. 4, pp. 61–76

Health Protection Scotland (2005) *Moving Forward: sexually transmitted infection, including HIV, in Scotland, 2005*, ISD Scotland Publications

Health Protection Scotland (2007) *Sexually Transmitted Infections and Other Sexual Health Information for Scotland*, ISD Scotland Publications

Heaphy, B. (2007) 'Sexualities, gender and ageing: resources and social change', *Current Sociology*, Vol. 55, No. 2, pp. 193–210

Heaphy, B. and Yip, A. (2003) 'Uneven possibilities: understanding non-heterosexual ageing and the implications of social change', *Sociological Research Online*, Vol. 8, No. 4. Available from URL: www.socresonline.org.uk/8/4/heaphy.html (accessed 12 July 2008)

Heaphy, B. and Yip, A. (2006) 'Policy implications of ageing sexualities', *Social Policy and Society*, Vol. 5, No. 4, pp. 443–51

Heaphy, B., Yip, A. and Thompson, D. (2003) *'Lesbian, Gay and Bisexual Lives over 50'*, A report on the project 'The Social and Policy Implications of Non-heterosexual Ageing', Nottingham: York House Publications

Heath, H. and White, I. (2007) *The Challenge of Sexuality in Health Care*, Oxford: Blackwell Science

Herdt, G. (ed.) (1998) *'Third Sex, Third Gender: Beyond Sexual Dimorphism in Culture and History*, New York: Zone Books

Hicks, S. (2008) 'Thinking through sexuality', *Journal of Social Work*, Vol. 8, No. 1, pp. 65–82

Hicks, S. and Watson, C. (2003) 'Desire lines: "queering" health and social welfare', *Sociological Research Online*, Vol. 8, No. 1. Available at URL: www.socresonline.org.uk/8/1/hicks.html (accessed 23 September 2007)

Hindle, P. (2001) 'The influence of the Gay Village on migration to central Manchester', *North West Geographer*, Vol. 3, No. 1, pp. 21–28

Hines, S. (2007) *TransForming Gender: Transgender Practices of Identity, Intimacy and Care*, Bristol: The Policy Press

Hubbard, R. and Rossington, J. (1995), *As We Grow Older: A Study of the Housing and Support Needs of Older Lesbians and Gay Men*, London: Polari. Available from URL: www.casweb.org/polari/file-storage/download/As%20We%20Grow%20Older.pdf?version_id=66608 (accessed 4 February 2008)

Hudspith, M. (1999), *Caring for Lesbian Health*, British Columbia: Ministry of Health and Ministry Responsible for Seniors. Available from URL: www.health.gov.bc.ca/library/publications/year/1999/caring.pdf (accessed 4 February 2008)

Hunt, R. and Dick, S. (2008) *Serves You Right: Lesbian and Gay People's Expectations of Discrimination*, London: Stonewall

Hunt, R. and Fish, J. (2008) *Prescription for Change: Lesbian and Bisexual Women's Health Check 2008*, London: Stonewall

Hunt, R. and Minsky, A. (2006), *Reducing Health Inequalities for Lesbian Gay and Bisexual People: Evidence of Health Care Needs*, London: Stonewall

Hunt, R., Cowan, K. and Chamberlain, B. (2007) *Being the Gay One: Experiences of Lesbian, Gay and Bisexual People Working in the Health and Social Care Sector*, London: Stonewall

Israel, G. E. and Tarver, D. E. (1997) *Transgender Care: Recommended Guidelines, Practical Information and Personal Accounts*, Philadelphia: Temple University Press

James, N. (1992) 'Care = organisation + physical labour + emotional labour', *Sociology of Health and Illness*, Vol. 14, No. 4, pp. 488–509

Jamieson, A. (2002) 'Theory and practice in social gerontology', in Jamieson, A. and Victor, C. R. (eds) (2002) *Researching Ageing and Later Life: The Practice of Social Gerontology*, Buckingham: Open University Press, pp. 7–20

Jorm, A. F., Korten, A. E., Rodgers, B., Jacomb, P. A. and Christensen, H. (2002) 'Sexual orientation and mental health: results from a community survey of young and middle-aged adults', *British Journal of Psychiatry*, Vol. 180, No. 5, pp. 423–27

Kauth, M. R. (2005) 'Revealing assumptions: explicating sexual orientation and promoting conceptual integrity', *Journal of Bisexuality*, Vol. 5, No. 4, pp. 79–106

Kavanagh, T. (2006) 'Hughes: I've had gay sex', *The Sun* (26 January 2006)

Kellas, J. G. (1989) *The Scottish Legal System* (4th edition), Cambridge: Cambridge University Press

Keogh, P., Dodds, C. and Henderson, L. (2004) *Working Class Gay Men: Redefining Community, Restoring Identity*, London: Sigma Research

Kimmel, D. C. (1978) 'Adult development and aging: a gay perspective', *Journal of Social Issues*, Vol. 34, pp. 113–30

King, M., McKeown, E., Warner, J., Ramsay, A., Johnson, K., Cort, C., Wright, L., Blizard, R. and Davidson, O. (2003) 'Mental health and quality of life of gay men and lesbians in England and Wales: controlled, cross-sectional study', *British Journal of Psychiatry*, Vol. 183, pp. 552–8

Kinsey, A. C., Pomeroy, W. B., Martin, C. E. and Gebhard, P. H. (1948) *Sexual Behavior in the Human Male*, London: W. B. Saunders and Co.

Kinsey, A. C., Pomeroy, W. B., Martin, C. E. and Gebhard, P. H. (1953) *Sexual Behavior in the Human Female*, London: W. B. Saunders and Co.

Kitchen, G. (2003) *Social care needs of older gay men and lesbians on Merseyside*, Southport: Sefton Pensioners Advocacy Centre

Klein, F. (1993) *The Bisexual Option*, New York: Haworth Press

Knocker, S. (2006) *'The Whole of Me: Meeting the Needs of Older Lesbians, Gay Men and Bisexuals Living in Care Homes and Extra Care Housing'*, London: Age Concern England

Knussen, C. and Flowers, P. (2007) 'Notification of syphilis test results by telephone: acceptability ratings in a community-based sample of Scottish gay men', *International Journal of STD & AIDS,* Vol.18, No.12, pp. 827–82

Knussen, C., Flowers, P. and Church, S. (2004) 'The intentions of gay men in taking an HIV test', *Culture, Health and Sexuality*, Vol. 6, No. 1, pp. 45–60

Kurdek, L. (2005) 'What do we know about lesbian and gay couples?', *Current Directions in Psychological Science*, Vol. 14, No. 5, pp. 251–4

Langley, J. (2001) 'Developing anti-oppressive empowering social work practice with older lesbian women and gay men', *British Journal of Social Work*, Vol. 31, No. 6, pp. 917–32

Latimer, J. (1997) 'Figuring identities: older people, medicine and time', in Jamieson, A., Harper, S. and Victor, C. R. (eds) (1997) *Critical Approaches to Ageing and Later Life,* Buckingham: Open University Press, pp. 143–59

Lawrence, A. (2006, June) 'Clinical and Theoretical Parallels Between Desire for Limb Amputation and Gender Identity Disorder', Archives of Sexual Behavior, Vol. 35, No. 3. Available from Transsexual Women's Resources, URL: www.annelawrence.com/publications/amputation-GID.pdf (accessed 12 August 2008)

Lee, A. (2005) 'The influence of life experiences on attitudes towards homosexuality, and their effects on the way gay men negotiate later life', *Generations Review,* Vol. 15, No. 4, pp. 13–17

Lee, A. (2007) '"I can't ask that!" Promoting discussion of sexuality and effective health service interactions with older non-heterosexual men', in Clarke, K., Maltby, T. and Kennett, P. (eds) (2007) *Social Policy Review 19: Analysis and Debate in Social Policy, 2007*, Bristol: Policy Press, pp. 127–50

Lee, H. (2007) 'Why sexual health promotion misses its audience. Men who have sex with men reading the texts', *Journal of Health Organization and Management,* Vol. 21, No. 2, pp. 205–19

Lee-Treweek, G. (1994) 'Bedroom abuse: the hidden work in a nursing home', *Generations Review,* Vol. 4, No.1, pp. 2–4

LGBT Youth (2003) *Live To Tell,* Gay Men's Health Scotland, Edinburgh: LGBT Youth

Macartney, J. and Garlick, H. (2008, July 29) 'Girls will be girls at the Beijing Olympics – sex tests will prove it' (online). Available at URL: www.timesonline.co.uk/tol/sport/ olympics/article4419301.ece (accessed 11August 2008)

Macdonald, B. and Rich, C. (1983) *Look Me in the Eye: Old Women, Aging and Ageism,* Denver, CO: Spinster Ink Books

MacKian, S., Bedri, N. and Lovel, H. (2004) 'Up the garden path and over the edge: where might health seeking behaviour take us?' *Health Policy and Planning,* Vol. 19, No. 3, pp. 137–46

Male Health. Available from URL: www.malehealth.co.uk/userpage1.cfm?item_id=2391

Malebranche, J. (2007) *Androphilia: Rejecting the Gay Identity, Reclaiming Masculinity,* Baltimore, USA: Scapegoat Publishing

Mallon, G. P. (ed.) (1999) *Social Services with Transgendered Youth,* New York: Harrington Park Press

Manthorpe, J. and Price, E. (2003) 'Out of the shadows', *Community Care,* 3–9 April, pp. 40–41

Manthorpe, J. and Price, E. (2005) 'Lesbian carers: personal issues and policy responses', *Social Policy and Society,* Vol. 5, No. 1, pp. 15–26

McLean, C. and O'Connor, W. (2003) *Sexual Orientation Research Phase Two: The Future of LGBT Research – Perspectives of Community Organisations,* National Centre for Social Research

McManus, S. (2003) *Sexual Orientation Research Phase One: A review of Methodological Approaches,* National Centre for Social Research

McMillan, A. (2006) 'The changing prevalence of hepatitis B virus infection among men who have sex with men who attended a sexually transmitted infections clinic in Edinburgh', *International Journal of STD & AIDS,* Vol.17, No. 4, pp. 254–6

MetLife (2006) *Out and Aging: The MetLife Study of Lesbian and Gay Baby Boomers,* Westport, CT: MetLife Mature Market Institute. Available from URL: www.asaging. org/networks/lgain/OutandAging.pdf (accessed 4 February 2008)

Metz, P. (1997) 'Staff development for working with lesbian and gay elders', *Journal of Gay and Lesbian Social Services,* Vol. 6, No. 1, pp. 35–44

Meyer, I. H. and Northridge, M. E. (2006) *The Health of Sexual Minorities: Public Health Perspectives on Lesbian, Gay, Bisexual and Transgender Populations,* New York: Springer

Milne, A., Hatzidimitriadou, E., Chryssanthopoulou, C. and Owen, T. (2001), *Caring in Later Life: Reviewing the Role of Older Carers (Executive Summary),* London: Help the Aged. Available from URL: www.helptheaged.org.uk/NR/rdonlyres/1DC9A27D-3531- 4394-ACB2-0C6E5D418AE9/0/caring_in_later_life.pdf (accessed 4 February 2008)

Moon, L. (2008) *Feeling Queer or Queer Feelings? Radical Approaches to Counselling Sex, Sexualities and Genders,* London: Routledge

Mulick, P. S. and Wright, L. W. (2002) 'Examining the existence of biphobia in the hetero- sexual and homosexual populations', *Journal of Bisexuality,* Vol. 2, No. 4, pp. 47–64

Namaste, V. K. (2000). *Invisible Lives: The Erasure of Transsexual and Transgendered People,* Chicago: University of Chicago Press

Nataf, Z. (1995) *Lesbians Talk Transgender*, London: Scarlet Press

New American Dimensions /Asterix Group (2007) 'Real World Lesbians and Gays' (online). Available from URL: www.retailwire.com/BrainTrust/ResourceDocs/ CABC3B3B-AEC2-F84A-2BC5C9427B2BB63A.PDF (accessed 11 June 2008)

Northedge, A. (2002) 'Organising excursions into specialist discourse communities: a sociocultural account of university teaching', in Wells, G. and Claxton, G. (eds) (2002) *Learning for Life in the Twenty-first Century: Sociocultural Perspectives on the Future of Education*, Oxford: Blackwell, pp. 252–64

Northmore, S., Ball, C. and Smith, A. (2005) 'Multiple identities in older age – a re-examination', Paper presented at 2005 National Council for Voluntary Organisations' 11th Researching the Voluntary Sector Conference, University of Warwick, 31 August – 1 September 2005

Ochs, R. (1996) 'Biphobia: it goes more than two ways', in Firestein, B. A. (ed.) *Bisexuality: The Psychology and Politics of an Invisible Minority*, Thousand Oaks: Sage

Ochs, R. (2007) 'What's in a name? Why women embrace or resist bisexual identity', in Firestein, B. A. (ed) (2007) *Becoming Visible: Counseling Bisexuals Across the Lifespan*, New York: Columbia University Press

Office for Public Service Information (OPSI) (2003) *The Employment Equality (Sexual Orientation) Regulations 2003*, HMSO (online). Available from URL: www.opsi.gov. uk/si/si2003/20031661.htm (accessed 22 August 2008)

Office for Public Service Information (OPSI) (2004a) *Gender Recognition Act 2004*, HMSO (online). Available from URL: www.opsi.gov.uk/acts/acts2004/ukpga_20040007_en_1 (accessed 22 August 2008)

Office for Public Service Information (OPSI) (2004b) *The Civil Partnership Act 2004*, HMSO (online). Available from URL: www.opsi.gov.uk/acts/acts2004/ukpga_20040033_en_1 (accessed 22 August 2008)

Office for Public Service Information (2004c) *National Health Service Reform (Scotland) Act 2004*, HMSO (online). Available from URL: www.opsi.gov.uk/legislation/scotland/ acts2004/asp_20040007_en_1 (accessed 22 August 2008)

Office for Public Service Information (OPSI) (2006) *Equality Act 2006*, HMSO (online). Available from URL: www.opsi.gov.uk/acts/acts2006/pdf/ukpga_20060003_en.pdf (accessed 22 August 2008)

Office for Public Service Information (OPSI) (2007) *The Equality Act (Sexual Orientation) Regulations 2007*, HMSO (online). Available from URL: www.opsi.gov.uk/si/si2007/ uksi_20071263_en_1 (accessed 22 August 2008)

Office for Public Service Information (OPSI) (2008) *The Sex Discrimination (Amendment of Legislation) Regulations 2008*, HMSO (online). Available from URL: www.opsi.gov. uk/si/si2008/uksi_20080963_en_1 (accessed 22 August 2008)

Official Journal of the European Communities: 2000/78/EC, *EU Gender Directive 2000* (online). Available from URL: http://ec.europa.eu/employment_social/news/2001/jul/ directive78ec_en.pdf (accessed 22 August 2008)

O'Keefe, T. and Fox, K. (eds) (2003) *Finding the Real Me: True Tales of Sex and Gender Diversity*, San Francisco: Wiley

OurStory Scotland (2008) (online). Available from URL: www.ourstoryscotland.org.uk/ (accessed 22 August 2008)

Page, E. (2007) 'Bisexual women's and men's experiences of psychotherapy', in Firestein, B. A. (ed.) (2007) *Becoming Visible: Counseling Bisexuals Across the Lifespan*, New York: Columbia University Press

Palmer, H. M. and Young, H. (2006) 'Dramatic increase in a single genotype of TRNG ciprofloxacin-resistant Neisseria gonorrhoeae isolates in men who have sex with men', *International Journal of STD & AIDS*, Vol.17, No. 4, pp. 254–6

Pawson, R., Boaz, A., Grayson, L., Long, A. and Barnes, C. (2003) 'Types and quality of knowledge in social care', *Knowledge Review*, London: Social Care Institute for Excellence

Petford, B. (2003) 'Power in the darkness: some thoughts on the marginalisation of bisexuality in psychological literature', *Lesbian and Gay Psychology Review*, Vol. 4, No. 2, pp. 5–13

Posner, R. A. (1995) *Aging and Old Age*, Chicago: University of Chicago Press

Press For Change (2008) *Legal Matters* (online). Available from URL: www.pfc.org.uk/node/294 (accessed 22 August 2008)

Price, E. (2005), 'All but invisible: older gay men and lesbians', *Nursing Older People*, Vol. 17, No. 4, pp. 16–18

Price, E. (2008) 'Pride or prejudice?: gay men, lesbians and dementia', *British Journal of Social Work*, Vol. 38, No. 7, pp. 1337–52

Prosser, J. (1998) *Second Skins: The Body Narratives of Transsexuality*, New York: Columbia University Press

Pugh, S., McCartney, W., Ryan, J. and the Older Lesbian, Gay Men, Bisexual and Transgendered People's Network (2007) *Moving Forward: Working with and for Older Lesbians, Gay Men, Bisexuals and Transgendered People*, Salford: University of Salford

Ray, R. E., (2004) 'Toward the croning of feminist gerontology', *Journal of Aging Studies*, Vol. 18, No. 1, pp.109–121

Riessman, C. K. (1993) *Narrative Analysis*, London: Sage

River, L. (2006) 'A feasibility study of the needs of older lesbians in Camden and surrounding boroughs', London: Polari (online). Available at URL: www.casweb.org/polari/file-storage/index?folder_id=117692&n_past_days=99999 (accessed 2 August 2008)

Robinson, N. (1998) 'People with HIV/AIDS: who cares?' *Journal of Advanced Nursing*, Vol. 28, No. 4, pp. 771–8

Rodriguez-Rust, P. C. (ed.) (2000) *Bisexuality in the United States: A Social Science Reader*, New York: Columbia University Press

Rodriguez-Rust, P. C. (2007) 'The construction and reconstruction of bisexuality: inventing and reinventing the self', in Firestein, B. A. (ed.) (2007) *Becoming Visible: Counseling Bisexuals Across the Lifespan*, New York: Columbia University Press

Rose, K. and Webb, C. (1998) 'Analyzing data: maintaining rigor in a qualitative study', *Qualitative Health Research*, Vol. 8, No. 4, pp. 556–62

Rosenfeld, D. (1999) 'Identity work among lesbian and gay elderly', *Journal of Aging Studies*, Vol. 13, No. 2, pp. 121–44

Rosenfeld, D. (2002) 'Identity careers of older gay men and lesbians', in Gubrium, J. F. and Holstein, J. A. (eds) (2002) *Ways of Aging*, Oxford: Blackwell, pp. 160–81

Rothblatt, M. (1995) *The Apartheid of Sex: A Manifesto on the Freedom of Gender*, London: Harper Collins

Roulstone, A., Hudson, V., Kearney, J., Martin, A. and Warren, J. (2006) *Working Together: Carer Participation in England, Wales and Northern Ireland*, London: Social Care Institute for Excellence. Available from URL: www.scie.org.uk/publications/position-papers/pp05.pdf (accessed 4 February 2008)

Rust, P. C. (1992) 'The politics of sexual identity: sexual attraction and behavior among lesbian and bisexual women', *Social Problems*, Vol. 39, No. 4, pp. 366–86

Rust, P. C. (1993) '"Coming out" in the age of social constructionism: sexual identity formation among lesbian and bisexual women', *Gender and Society*, Vol. 7, No. 1, pp. 50–77

Rust, P. C. (1995) *Bisexuality and the challenge to lesbian politics*, New York: New York University Press

Scottish Executive (2000) *Adults with Incapacity (Scotland) Act*, HMSO

Scottish Executive (2001a) *Housing (Scotland) Act 2001*, HMSO

Scottish Executive (2001b) *Mortgage Rights (Scotland) Act 2001*, HMSO

Scottish Executive (2001c) *Patient Focus and Public Involvement*, HMSO

Scottish Executive (2003a) *Civil Legal Aid (Scotland) Amendment Regulations*, HMSO

Scottish Executive (2003b) *Criminal Justice (Scotland) Act 2003*, HMSO

Scottish Executive (2003c) *Mental Health (Care and Treatment) (Scotland) Act*, HMSO

Scottish Executive (2003d) *'Partnership for Care': Scotland's Health White Paper*, HMSO

Scottish Executive (2003e) 'Working Group on Hate Crime' (online). Available from URL: www.scotland.gov.uk/about/JD/CJ/00017915/wg_papers.aspx (accessed 25 June 2009)

Scottish Executive (2005) *Equality and Diversity Impact Assessment Toolkit* (online). Available from URL: www.scotland.gov.uk/Publications/2005/02/20687/52421 (accessed 22 August 2008)

Scottish Executive (2006a) *Adoption and Children (Scotland) Bill*, HMSO

Scottish Executive (2006b) *Family Law (Scotland) Act*, Edinburgh: The Stationery Office

Scottish Executive Health Department (2004) 'Fair For All – The Wider Challenge' (online). Available from URL: www.sehd.scot.nhs.uk/publications/ffaleaflet.pdf (accessed 22 August 2008)

Scottish Government (2007) *Attitudes to discrimination in Scotland: 2006*, Edinburgh: Scottish Government Social Research

Scottish Government (2008a) 'Challenging Prejudice: Changing Attitudes towards Lesbian, Gay, Bisexual and Transgender People in Scotland' (Recommendations of the LGBT Hearts and Minds Agenda Group) (online). Available at URL: www.scotland.gov.uk/Publications/2008/02/19133153/0 (accessed 2 September 2008)

Scottish Government (2008b) *PRIME: Portal to Resources and Information on Mainstreaming Equality* (online). Available from URL: www.scotland.gov.uk/Topics/People/Equality/18507/mainstreamingequalities (accessed 3 June 2008)

Scottish Parliament (2008) *Offences (Aggravation by Prejudice) (Scotland) Bill (SP Bill 09)* (online). Available from URL: www.scottish.parliament.uk/s3/bills/09-AggPrej/index.htm (accessed 22 August 2008)

Scottish Public Health Observatory, www.scotpho.org.uk

Scottish Transgender Alliance / Equality Network (2008) *Transgender Experiences in Scotland* (online). Available from URL: www.scottishtrans.org/Uploads/Resources/staexperiencessummary03082.pdf (accessed 12 June 2009)

Seidman, S. (1996) 'Introduction', in Seidman S. (ed.) *Queer Theory/Sociology*, Oxford: Blackwell, pp. 1–29

Shokeid, M. (2001) 'You don't eat Indian and Chinese food at the same meal: the bisexual quandary', *Anthropological Quarterly*, Vol. 75, No. 1, pp. 63–90

Simpson, M. (1999) 'Here come the mirror men', *The Independent*, 15 November 1994 (online). Available from URL: www.marksimpson.com/pages/journalism/mirror_men.html (accessed 22 August 2008)

Skeggs, B. (1999) 'Matter out of place: visibility and sexualities in leisure spaces', *Leisure Studies*, Vol. 18, pp. 213–32

Skeggs, B. (2004) *Class, Self, Culture,* London: Routledge

Smiley, E. B. (1997) 'Counselling bisexual clients', *Journal of Mental Health Counselling*, Vol. 19, No. 4, pp. 373–82

Spanner Trust (2008) (online). Available from URL: www.spannertrust.org/documents/spannerhistory.asp (accessed 22 August 2008)

Stone, S. (1991) 'The empire strikes back: a posttranssexual manifesto', in Epstein, J. and Straub, K. (eds) (1991) *Body Guards: The Cultural Politics of Gender Ambiguity*, New York: Routledge

Stonewall Cymru and Triangle Wales (2006) 'The Housing Needs of Lesbian, Gay and Bisexual (LGB) People in Wales', Cardiff: Welsh Assembly. Available from URL: www.stonewallcymru.org.uk/documents/triangle_wale__report_engli.pdf (accessed 4 April 2008)

Stonewall (2003) *Towards a Healthier LGBT Scotland*, NHS Inclusion Project, Glasgow: Stonewall/NHS Scotland

Swinton, J. (2001) *Spirituality in Mental Health Care*, London: Jessica Kingsley Publishers

Thomas, C. (1993) 'De-constructing concepts of care', *Sociology*, Vol. 27, No. 4, pp. 649–69

Thompson, N. (1998) *Promoting Equality: Challenging Discrimination and Oppression in the Human Services*, London: MacMillan

Tully, B. (1992) *Accounting for Transsexualism and Transhomosexuality*, London: Whiting and Birch

Turnbull, A. (2001) *Opening Doors: A Literature Review,* London: Age Concern England

Udis-Kessler, A. (1995) 'Identity/politics: a history of the bisexual movement', in Tucker, N. (ed.) (1995) *Bisexual Politics: Theories, Queries, and Visions*, New York: The Haworth Press, pp.17–30

Valentine, G. (1993) 'Negotiating and managing multiple sexual identities: lesbian time-space strategies', *Transactions of the Institute of British Geographers, New Series*, Vol. 18, No. 2, pp. 237–48

Vines, G. (1992) 'Last Olympics for the sex test?', *New Scientist*, 4 July 1992 (online). Available at URL: www.newscientist.com/article/mg13518284.900-last-olympics-for-the-sex-test-the-worlds-biggest-sportsbody-has-just-banned-sex-tests-branding-them-unfair-and-unnecessary-butthe-old-guard-at-this-years-olympics-still-insists-the-practice-must-goon.htm (accessed 13 August 2008)

Wanless, D. (2004) *Securing Good Health for the Whole Population*, London: HM Treasury

Ward, R., River, L. and Fenge, L. (2008) 'Neither silent nor invisible: a comparison of two participative projects involving older lesbians and gay men in the United Kingdom', *Journal of Gay and Lesbian Social Services*, Vol. 20, No.1–2, pp. 147–65

Ward, R., Jones, R., Hughes, J., Humberstone, N. and Pearson, R. (2008) 'Intersections of ageing and sexuality: accounts from older people', in Ward, R. and Bytheway, B. (eds) *Researching Age and Multiple Discrimination,* London: Centre for Policy on Ageing, pp. 45–72

Ward, R., Vass, A. A., Aggarwal, N., Garfield, C. and Cybyk, B. (2005) 'A kiss is still a kiss? The construction of sexuality in dementia care', *Dementia*, Vol. 4, No. 1, pp. 49–72

Warner, J., McKeown, E., Griffin, M., Ramsay, A., Johnson, K., Cort, C. and King, M. (2004) 'Rates and predictors of mental illness in gay men, lesbians and bisexual men and women: results from a survey based in England and Wales', *British Journal of Psychiatry*, Vol.185, No. 6, pp. 479–85

Warner, M. (1991) 'Introduction: fear of a queer planet', *Social Text*, Vol. 29, No. 4, pp. 3–17

Warnke, G. (2007) *After Identity: Rethinking Race, Sex, and Gender*, Cambridge: Cambridge University Press

Webb, C. (1992) 'The use of the first person in academic writing: objectivity, language and gatekeeping', *Journal of Advanced Nursing*, Vol. 17, No. 6, pp. 747–52

Webb, T. (1996) 'Autobiographical fragments from a transsexual activist', in Ekins, R. and King, D. (eds) (1996) *Blending Genders: Social Aspects of Cross-dressing and Sex-changing*, London: Routledge

Weeks, J. (1995) *Invented Moralities: Sexual Values in an Age of Uncertainty*, Bristol: Polity Press

Weinberg, M. S., Williams, C. J. and Pryor, D. W. (2001) 'Bisexuals at midlife: commitment, salience and identity', *Journal of Contemporary Ethnography*, Vol. 30, No. 2, pp. 180–208

Weitzman, G. (2007) 'Counseling bisexuals in polyamorous relationships', in Firestein, B. A. (ed.) (2007) *Becoming Visible: Counseling Bisexuals Across the Lifespan*, New York: Columbia University Press

Whittaker, T. (1995) 'Violence, gender and elder abuse: towards a feminist analysis and practice', *Journal of Gender Studies*, Vol. 4, No. 1, pp. 35–45

Whittle, S., Turner, L. and Al-Alami, M. (2007) *Engendered Penalties: Transgender and Transsexual People's Experiences of Inequality and Discrimination*, The Equalities Review / Press for Change / Manchester Metropolitan University

Whyte, C. (ed.) (1995) *Gendering the Nation: Studies in Modern Scottish Literature*, Edinburgh: Edinburgh University Press

Williamson, L. M. and Hart, G. J. (2007) 'HIV prevalence and undiagnosed infection among a community sample of gay men in Scotland', *Journal of Acquired Immune Deficiency Syndrome*, Vol. 45, No. 2, pp. 224–30

Williamson, L. M., Dodds, J. P., Mercey, D. E., Hart, G. J. and Johnson, A. M. (2008) 'Sexual risk behaviour and knowledge of HIV status among community samples of gay men in the UK', *AIDS*, Vol. 22, pp. 1063–70

Wilton, T. (2000) *Sexualities in Health and Social Care: A Textbook*, Buckingham: Open University Press

Yamey, G. (2003) 'Gay tobacco ads come out of the closet', *British Medical Journal*, Vol. 327, No. 7409, p. 296

Yirrell, D. L., Shaw, L., Burns, S. M., Cameron, S. O., Quigg, M., Campbell, E. and Goldberg, D. (2004) 'HIV-1 subtype in Scotland: the establishment of a national surveillance system', *Epidemiology and Infection*, Vol.132, No. 4, pp. 693–8

Young, H., McElhinney, J. and Palmer, H. M. (2006) 'Extended surveillance of gonorrhoea in Scotland 2003', *International Journal of STD & AIDS*, Vol.17, No.10, pp. 687–92

Index